DEEP AWAKE is an inspirational guide to spiritual awakening based on Tim Freke's *The Mystery Experience*.

TIM FREKE is a pioneering philosopher and respected authority on ancient and contemporary spirituality, whose work has touched the lives of hundreds of thousands of people worldwide. He is the author of more than 20 books, which have been translated into 15 languages, including an international bestseller and *Daily Telegraph* 'Book of the Year'. He presents life-changing events internationally and online. He has often been featured in the global media, including the BBC and the History Channel.

GUIDED MEDITATIONS

You can download audio versions of the guided meditations in this book from www.TimFreke.com

DEEP AWAKE

WAKE UP TO ONENESS AND CELEBRATE YOUR INDIVIDUALITY

T!M FREKE

WATKINS

Sharing Wisdom Since
1893

DEEP AWAKE
T!M FREKE

This edition first published in the UK and USA 2016 by Watkins,
an imprint of Watkins Media Limited.
19 Cecil Court
London WC2N 4EZ
enquiries@watkinspublishing.com

1 3 5 7 9 10 8 6 4 2

Designed and typeset by Barnaby Adams

Printed and bound in Finland

A CIP record for this book is available from the British Library

ISBN: 978-1-78028-986-1

www.watkinspublishing.com

CHAPTER 1

DEEP AWAKE

What we experience depends on how conscious we are. When we only pay attention to the surface of life we're only superficially awake, but when we look deeper we can become deep awake. This feels like waking up from a semi-conscious trance and remembering we are alive. We become conscious of how profoundly mysterious life really is. We feel present in the moment and filled with wonder. Then, if we really immerse ourselves in the deep awake state, life becomes WOW!

Recently I dreamed I was standing on a stage about to talk to a large audience about becoming deep awake, as I often do in my waking life. Before I started to talk I paused, because I couldn't find the words to express how wonderful it feels. Then suddenly I knew what to do, because I remembered that I could fly!

So I simply said, 'Being deep awake feels like this' …
and I soared up into the air … dancing ecstatically in
the emptiness of space … swooping up and down in
effortless abandon.

I wish I could swoop and dive for you right now,
to convey how it feels to be deep awake, but I haven't
worked out how to fly in waking life. And this is a book
so you wouldn't see me anyway. That means I'll have
to describe it in words for you as best I can. I know that
won't be easy, but I'm going to give it a go.

When I am deep awake it feels as if I'm dissolving
in an ocean of love. There's an awe-inspiring sense of
oneness with the universe. My sensual body comes
alive. The search for meaning is resolved into a wordless
'understanding', which is so deep it must be felt not
thought. There's the silent certainty that all is well. And
such a feeling of relief … like coming home.

THE WOW OF AWAKENING

I've been exploring the deep awake state since I
experienced an unexpected awakening when I was a
12-year-old boy. Over the decades I've had the privilege
of being with many people when they've found
themselves in the awakened state for the first time.

And the most common thing that people say is simply 'WOW'.

The Deep Awakening is a transformative retreat I have presented around the world for many years, during which I guide people directly to the deep awake state. Afterwards I receive a large number of moving emails from participants and, again, by far the most used word is 'WOW', which is usually in capital letters followed by a string of exclamation marks!!!

I like the word 'wow'. I think of it as modern American slang, but my dictionary tells me it's a natural expression that originated in 16th century Scotland. 'Wow' is a way of expressing astonishment and wonder. It's a great word to describe how it feels when we awaken, because becoming deep awake is a very big WOW.

Perhaps there have been moments in your life when you tasted the WOW of awakening? Most of us, at one time or another, have found ourselves suddenly seeing through the superficialities of life and diving into the mysterious depths. This can happen when we embrace a newborn child … or listen to beautiful music … or enjoy a deep conversation. It can happen when we confront death … or feel defeated by failure … or wrestle with a mental breakdown. It can happen at any time. It can happen now.

At the end of a *Deep Awakening* retreat in Las Vegas, while we luxuriated together in the wonder of the WOW, people attempted to describe what they were experiencing in various ways. Then a lovely woman called Kate said:

> This is what everyone wants to feel.

I love that description of the awakened state, because it's so simple and so true. Being deep awake is the WOW that everyone is searching for. We all long to feel alive and when we awaken we feel totally alive. We all long for freedom and when we awaken we know that we're completely free. We all long for love and when we awaken we become immersed in limitless love.

Experiencing the deep awake state is traditionally called 'spiritual awakening', but you don't need to think of yourself as 'spiritual' to experience the WOW. It is natural and available to all of us. It's available to you.

Spirituality is often misunderstood as a way of thinking about life, but first and foremost it's a guide to transforming consciousness and *experiencing* something beyond words. Zen Master Daie put it perfectly, nearly a thousand years ago, when he wrote:

> All the teachings the sages have expounded are no more than commentaries on the sudden cry … Ah, this!

So let me plagiarize old man Daie and say right now:

> All the ideas in this book are just commentaries on the joyous whoop … WOW! This is it!

I remember many years ago, at one of my very first retreats, a young woman arrived dressed all in black and feeling very withdrawn. At the end, beaming and brimming with love, she announced:

> I feel like a convert to … *something*.

Yes! That's it. I'm also a convert to *something*. In this book I want to invite you to experience the WOW and become a convert to *something!*

CHAPTER 2

21ST CENTURY SPIRITUALITY

Over the last four decades I've studied and written many books about the major spiritual traditions of the world. These different approaches to awakening have all influenced me profoundly and I feel immense gratitude to those great spiritual explorers who've cleared a way for me through the bewilderment of life.

I love the simple naturalness of Taoism, the searing immediacy of Zen, the ecstatic devotion of Sufism, the philosophical depth of Advaita Vedanta, the expansive love of Christianity, the esoteric wisdom of Kabala, the magical earthiness of Shamanism. All these traditions and many others have touched me in different ways. But I don't see myself as part of any particular spiritual tradition, because I prefer to draw on all the wisdom of the world.

In recent years I've been articulating a new philosophy of awakening. In my view spirituality, like everything else, needs to keep evolving. So I've felt inspired to create a new approach to spirituality for the 21st century, which has all the depth of the traditions I've studied, yet avoids some of the dead ends I've been down on my own journey of awakening.

It seems to me that to be relevant to our modern world a new philosophy of awakening must distance itself from the irrational dogmas of outdated religion. We need to find new ways to express the great insights of spirituality, so that they sit comfortably alongside and complement the awesome discoveries of modern science.

Many new approaches to spirituality are evolving at the moment and my work is a contribution to that movement. Some are deep and promising, but many seem superficial and confused. A spiritual philosophy for the 21st century needs to be clear and simple, so that it points us beyond words to the actual experience of awakening. But I find some modern spirituality to be simplistic rather than simple. As that wonderfully awake scientist Albert Einstein once remarked, we should make things 'as simple as possible, but no simpler'.

HUMAN-CENTRED SPIRITUALITY

It seems to me that a new spirituality for the 21st century needs to be emphatically human-centred and radically world-embracing. It needs to help us live our everyday lives in a deeper and more enlivened way, rather than offering an otherworldly escape.

In the past spiritual traditions have often been very negative about the human experience. They portray the world we inhabit as an illusion from which we need to wake up by becoming enlightened, so we don't have to reincarnate back into this troublesome human existence. That's why 'real' spiritual seekers renounce the world and become monks.

The individual self, often pejoratively referred to as the 'ego', is an inner enemy that works to prevent us from awakening. Most of the characteristics that define our humanity are bad and must be avoided. Thinking is bad. Emotional attachments are bad. Desires are bad. Our humanity prevents us waking up.

I don't resonate with this negative spirituality at all. When I'm deep awake the world becomes wonderland. When I wake up to oneness I don't want to relinquish my human individuality, I want to celebrate it. When I become immersed in deep love I don't want to withdraw from life, I want to passionately enter into life to share the love.

In many spiritual traditions the body is a burden, a prison for the soul and a source of suffering. But when I'm deep awake there is a visceral love of being that permeates this amazing skin-bag of nerves, meat and bones I call my body. Hurray for the body! Everybody should have one!

For some spiritual traditions the mind is a problem, distracting us from quiet devotion and making us doubt the received wisdom of the masters. But when I'm deep awake I delight in my ability to question deeply and think clearly. New insights continually transform my experience of living in unexpected ways. To me the mind is a miracle, not a monster.

Negative spirituality encourages us to be detached from the world and focus on self-realization. A new spirituality for the 21st century needs to be about both self-realization and self-expression. I want to champion a world-embracing spirituality that urges 'know yourself and show yourself'. I want us to wake up to oneness so we can more fully contribute to life as unique individuals.

FROM ME TO YOU

I'm writing this book because I want to share with you what I've learned about becoming deep awake. It's full of big ideas that can change the way you understand your life and some powerful practices to take you beyond words, so that you actually experience the deep awake state for yourself.

First I want to introduce you to some new concepts, including an innovative 'both/and' approach to thinking, which will make profound spiritual ideas easily accessible.

Then we'll set out to answer the great spiritual question, 'Who am I?' and explore the profound paradox of our identity.

This will lead us to become conscious of the oneness of being and feel the all-embracing love that naturally arises in the deep awake state.

Finally we can return to our everyday lives, but seeing them now with exquisite new depth, so that we really appreciate the human adventure.

A book is inevitably a one-way conversation, but I don't want this to be a lecture. I'd much prefer it to feel like a 'tête à tête' or better still a 'heart to heart'. I want to connect with you in the most authentic way I can, because when we're real with each other magic happens.

As I write this book I want to reach through the page to touch you. And, as you read this book, I want you to never forget that these are more than words on a page. As the American poet Walt Whitman writes:

> Camerado! This is no book,
> Who touches this, touches a man,
> (Is it night? Are we here together alone?)
> It is I you hold, and who holds you …

We're in different places in the web of space-time, but we're together here and now nevertheless. So let me tell you a bit about myself. I want to be upfront about something important right from the start. Just because I'm a teacher of spiritual awakening doesn't mean I see myself as some sort of enlightened master. I'm simply a human being with a passion for exploring the depths of life.

My journey of awakening hasn't led me to arrive at some 'fully realized' state. Indeed these days I neither expect nor aspire to be enlightened. And that isn't an admission of spiritual failure, because I've come to feel the whole idea of special enlightened people is completely misconceived.

I've written a lot of books on spiritual philosophy, but I still feel like a child taking my first teetering steps. How else could I feel in the face of the infinite mystery of life? I'm not claiming I have privileged knowledge of the way things are. It's simply that I've spent my life exploring the deep awake state.

But this doesn't mean my life is always perfect. It is full of highs and lows, just as I suspect your life is. I'm writing these words to connect with you precisely because we share the same dilemmas. We're all in the mystery of life together, and I want to offer to you what I've found of value, in gratitude for all that I've been given.

THE BIG QUESTION AND THE BIG ANSWER

If you're intrigued to learn more about my personal journey of awakening, then check out my book *How Long Is Now?*, which is full of anecdotes and stories. There's no time for all that now, because we've got a very big adventure ahead of us. But before we set off I feel it may be helpful to share with you how my personal journey began.

As a boy I found it very strange that all the grown-ups were preoccupied with trivia and never seemed to mention how profoundly mysterious existence is. Life seemed like one big question and I felt intuitively sure there must be a big answer. I would often sit quietly and wonder, because I figured that if I could work out what life is, then I'd know what I should be doing with it.

My favourite place to wonder was on Summerhouse Hill overlooking my busy little home town in the West Country of England. One day, sitting there consumed by the mystery of life, something magical happened. My state of consciousness spontaneously transformed. I became deep awake for the first time and it was WOW!

It's a long time ago but I can still vividly recall the feeling of being immersed in overwhelming love. It felt as if the whole universe was pulsating with limitless love. It felt as if I was dissolving into this love and becoming one with everything. It felt like I'd been given the most amazing surprise. And yet it also felt as if I'd remembered something I'd always secretly known.

I had no way of understanding what was happening to me, but I knew that I'd found the big answer to the big question of life. And the answer was not a clever theory. It was an amazing experience in which the big question dissolved into an ocean of love. This discovery changed my life.

Ever since that moment I've been exploring the deep awake state. I've continually experimented with ways to transform consciousness and be more awake in my everyday life. But my spiritual journey hasn't brought me to a permanently awakened state in which I am always blissful and my life is perfect, as I once hoped it would.

Something more amazing has happened. I've fallen in love with my tender, vulnerable, wounded humanity … just as it is … in all its glorious ambiguity. I've fallen in love with my wonderful, terrifying, everyday life … just as it is … in all its bittersweet splendour.

CHAPTER 3

A NEW LANGUAGE OF AWAKENING

To create a spirituality for the 21st century I've developed a new language of awakening. The concepts we use matter, because the way we think conditions what we experience. The WOW is beyond words, but the words we use have a huge effect on how we approach the journey of awakening.

I've loved studying the spiritual traditions of the world and have immense respect for the wisdom they've bequeathed us as our heritage. But traditional spiritual vocabulary comes from a different time and culture, so it can often be extremely confusing. In my experience this can mean that spiritual ideas we adopt to help us understand the depths of life often actually prevent us seeing how natural it is to simply awaken.

So I've set out to develop new concepts that can help us explore a new way to the WOW. Lucid concepts that cast the perennial insights of spirituality in a fresh light. Living concepts that speak the language of today. Truthful concepts that authentically capture my own experience of the deep awake state.

I've already introduced you to my concepts of 'deep awake' and the 'WOW'. Now I want to introduce you to more concepts that I use to describe the awakened state, which are like signposts that point to the wordless awakening from different directions. Read the signs and then look where they're pointing.

The Deep Mystery

I find it helpful to imagine life as a great ocean. When I *only* pay attention to the surface of life I feel as if I know who I am and what my existence is all about. I have a superficial understanding of life, which allows me to navigate my everyday world. But when I reach below the surface of things, right down to the depths of life, I realize that I really don't understand what life is at all … and I find myself immersed in the 'deep mystery'.

The deep mystery isn't a mystery that we could one day solve, such as 'Is there life on Mars?' The deep mystery is the ultimate mystery of existence. The deep mystery is the primal mystery that the universe exists and we are here to think about it. It's the great mystery in which we live and breathe and have our being. And when we become conscious of the deep mystery ... the deep awake state begins to spontaneously arise.

Deep Knowing

Paradoxically, when I'm immersed in the deep mystery I find myself *knowing* something. But this isn't 'knowing' in the normal sense in which I know certain information about the world. It's a more profound knowing than that, so I call it 'deep knowing'.

In the western spiritual tradition this 'deep knowing' is called *gnosis.* Gnosis is directly knowing the essence of things. It's the big answer to the big question of life. But this answer is not in the form of a collection of words. It's an immediate realization unmediated by concepts. It's like having the most profound thought you've ever had ... only without the thought.

Deep knowing transforms my experience of living, because it gives rise to a quiet confidence that, despite appearances, life is good. When I become deep awake, I have an unshakable faith that fundamentally all is well. Even when things are rough on the surface, at the depths of life I experience a primal joy of being.

The Deep I

When I become deep awake I see that I am much more than the person I appear to be on the surface of life. There's a deeper level to my identity that I call the 'deep I'. When I bob along on the surface of life I don't notice the deep I, but it's always there. The deep I is a permanent presence witnessing the ever-changing dramas of my personal self.

The personal self is what I appear to be. I appear to be 'Tim'. But the deep I is what I *am* … my mysterious essence … my ineffable spirit … my naked *being*. And when I become conscious of my deepest being I discover I am one with all *beings*. I see that as separate individuals you and I are like different waves on one great ocean of being.

Deep Love

When I know I'm essentially one with all, there is a profound sense of connectedness to life that I experience as all-encompassing love. Christians call this love *agape* and Buddhists call it *metta*. I call it 'deep love' because it spontaneously arises in the deep awake state. In my previous books I've also called it 'big love', because this love is so very big.

This profound connectedness could also be described as 'compassion' and 'kindness', but I particularly like the word 'love' because it's such a *feeling* word … and deep love is an exquisite feeling that reaches right down into my body. It's the feeling that arises when I am conscious that I am essentially one with all.

Love is always an experience of communing as one through the separateness that divides us. When we love someone we share in their joy and suffering. We feel separate and not separate from each other. We become conscious of the intimate depths of our connectedness. And that feels good.

In the same way, when I become conscious of the intimate depths of my connectedness to all of life, I find myself in love with life. When I know that I'm separate and not separate from everything and everyone, I find myself in love with everything and everyone. And that feels very good indeed.

A LOVER OF LIFE

When I'm deep awake I become a 'lover of life'. Some spiritual traditions suggest that the goal of the spiritual journey is to eradicate the ego and become enlightened. This is a permanent state of detached equanimity and contentment in which we are untouched by the vicissitudes of life. My concept of being a lover of life is a radically different alternative spiritual ideal.

Being a lover of life doesn't mean always feeling life is wonderful. It means loving life as it is. We need to regularly experience the ecstasy of being alive, because otherwise we become joyless and numb. But life is a transformative process that involves a vast spectrum of experiences.

Being a lover of life means embracing both the good and bad of life. It means passionately enjoying and tenderly enduring the tumultuous adventure of life through which we learn how to love. And it means understanding that to love deeply is sometimes to suffer deeply.

A few years ago my mum died of cancer. For the previous eight months I had watched this beautiful, vibrant woman, full of goodness and giving, lose control of her body and fade away. It broke my heart because I love her. Being deep awake didn't stop me suffering and I didn't want it to. I *wanted* to suffer with my mum. I wanted to be right with her in the horror of the situation.

For me awakening isn't about avoiding suffering, as some spiritual traditions teach. Rather it allows me to suffer willingly because of love. And then my heartbreak becomes poignant … meaningful … even beautiful. When I suffered with my dying mum there were precious moments of deep connection and utter magic. The bitterness was also sweet. The deep pain plunged me down to the depths of life. It broke my heart and what poured out was a deeper love.

Being deep awake feels good, but it's not just a good feeling. It is much deeper than that. It's appreciating the WOW that is always present in all life's ever-changing moods. The ecstatic WOW of elation and the subdued WOW of sadness. The intoxicating WOW of hope and the sobering WOW of disappointment. The warm WOW of intimacy and the piercing WOW of loss. The great song of life passes between the major and the minor modes … and when I'm deep awake I am stirred by both.

CHAPTER 4

PARALOGICAL THINKING

The 21st century spirituality I want to share with you has its philosophical foundation in what I call 'paralogical thinking'. This may seem abstract at first, but it has far-reaching practical applications. It opens up an understanding of the depths of life and clears away the confusion that can prevent us from becoming deep awake.

Normal 'logical' thinking says that a statement is either true or false. Paralogical thinking is based on an understanding that statements can be *both* true *and* false, depending on how we look at them, because life is profoundly paradoxical.

The great psychologist Carl Jung contrasted what he called the 'parsimonious either/or' with the 'glorious both/and'. This is a simple way of differentiating logical and paralogical thinking:

Logical thinking is either/or thinking.

Paralogical thinking is both/and thinking.

We don't have to choose between *either* logical thinking *or* paralogical thinking. They can both help us understand life. We need to use logical thinking when we're dealing with surface matters and paralogical thinking when we want to understand life in more depth.

Here's an everyday example of paralogical thinking: If I say to you, 'I watched the sunrise this morning', that happens to be true. But if I also say, 'Actually the sun never rises, because planet earth is a sphere orbiting the sun', this is also true. So I *both* did *and* didn't watch the sun rise … depending on how you look at it. For most purposes it would be enough simply to say it is true I watched the sunrise, but understanding how this is also not true adds depth to my understanding.

Here's a mind-blowing example of paralogical thinking from quantum physics. When physicists studied the nature of light they discovered that if an experiment is set up in one way, light appears to be comprised of elementary particles, but if the experiment is set up in another way, light appears to behave as a wave. So is light a wave or particles?

Niels Bohr, one of the founding fathers of quantum physics, arrived at the principle of 'complementarity' to answer this question. He understood the paradoxical nature of reality and so came to believe that light can be seen as *both* a wave *and* particles, depending on how you look at it. These two opposite perspectives are complementary to each other and we need both in order to fully understand the paradoxical nature of reality. Physicists call this paradox the 'wave–particle duality'.

In this book I want to explore a paralogical approach to awakening. Most spiritual traditions are stuck in either/or thinking. For example, one of the big revelations of the WOW is that at the depths of our being all is one. Either/or thinking says that we face a choice between experiencing *either* our human individuality *or* the deep oneness of being. I'm going to suggest that if we think paralogically we'll see that we can experience *both* oneness *and* separateness at the same time. They are opposite but complementary perspectives and we need to embrace both to fully understand the paradoxical nature of life.

PARALOGICAL VISION

It's interesting to consider why we look at the world with two eyes, rather than one big eye in the middle of the forehead like a Cyclops. The reason for this is that if we had only one eye we'd perceive a flat world. Looking at things with two eyes is what enables us to perceive depth. This is a great analogy for paralogical thinking.

> Logical, either/or thinking is like looking out of one eye or the other.

> Paralogical, both/and thinking is like looking out of both eyes.

When we look at the world what each eye sees is different, but they combine to create a single vision of reality that has depth. In the same way when we think paralogically we see things from two complementary perspectives at once and this gives depth to our understanding of life.

I call that single vision a 'paradoxity'. We see the paradoxity of something when we understand it from two opposite perspectives at once. For example, the paradoxity of my experience this morning is that I did and didn't watch the sun rise. The paradoxity of light is that it appears as a wave and as particles, depending on how you set up the experiment.

From the logical perspective paradoxes are problems to be solved. But paralogical thinking allows us to embrace paradox. Indeed, rather than try to avoid paradoxes, we seek to understand the paradoxity of whatever we are thinking about. Niels Bohr once famously remarked:

> How wonderful that we have met with a paradox. Now we have some hope of making progress.

THE PRIMAL PARADOX

Niels Bohr was a very interesting man. He was one of the most influential scientists of all time and a winner of a Nobel Prize for physics. Yet when he designed his own coat of arms he chose to put on it a spiritual symbol from ancient China. This symbol is commonly known as the yin/yang, but it is properly called the *taijitu,* which means 'diagram of the supreme ultimate'. Now there's a big claim to live up to!

The *taijitu* is a symbolic representation of the paradoxical nature of reality. It encodes the ancient Taoist understanding that reality is characterized by the primal polarity of yin and yang, represented by black and white 'tadpoles'.

Yin and yang are opposites that paradoxically co-exist and complement each other. This is why there's a dot of white in the black 'tadpole' and vice versa.

It's astonishing how the *taijitu* diagram anticipates the discovery of the wave–particle duality. If you place the symbol on its side, it creates the image of a wave flanked by two particles, one of which is white and the other black. This is quite extraordinary because physics has now found that all elementary particles come into existence with a complementary anti-particle of opposite charge, forming negative and positive pairs.

Niels Bohr clearly felt the yin/yang symbol captured the paradoxical understanding of reality he had arrived at through his scientific discoveries. And he made this plain, by adding on his coat of arms a Latin motto:

Contraria sunt complementa

Opposites are complementary

This is an idea that has been important to many of the greatest philosophers, who often referred to it as the *coincidentia oppositorum* or 'union of opposites'. The essential idea is that existence is a primal oneness that manifests itself as complementary opposites.

SCIENCE AND SPIRITUALITY

In the 21st century we need an approach to spirituality that can sit comfortably alongside science. Paralogical thinking can help us see that science and spirituality offer opposite but complementary ways of understanding reality.

Science is an objective enquiry that entails looking out onto the world and asking 'what is it?' Spirituality is a subjective enquiry that entails looking within and asking 'who am I?' Science gives us the it-perspective on reality. Spirituality gives us the complementary I-perspective, which we will be focusing on in this book.

My previous book *The Mystery Experience,* on which this book is based, includes an in-depth exploration of the paralogical relationship between science and spirituality. It shows that many of the eminent scientists responsible for creating our modern worldview found that their scientific discoveries pushed them towards also embracing a mystical understanding of reality. This is a great surprise to most people, because we tend to think of science and mysticism as two opposing camps. But the greatest scientists and the greatest mystics don't think in this either/or way.

Wolfgang Pauli, a Nobel Prize-winning physicist and friend of Carl Jung, writes:

> I consider the ambition of overcoming opposites, so we can embrace both rational understanding and the mystical experience of unity, to be the challenge of our present age.

CHAPTER 5

THE DEEP MYSTERY

In the normal waking state we pay attention to the surface of life. Deep awakening happens when we look deeper. You can taste the deep awake state right now by simply becoming conscious of a simple paradoxity:

> We do and do not know what is going on.

On the one hand we understand more and more about life all the time. But isn't it also true that life remains a breathtaking mystery? Explore the mystery of this moment with me. I'll describe what I'm experiencing and you see if it's the same for you:

> I'm experiencing a tapestry of shapes and colours that I call the 'world' … but what is the world?

I'm experiencing thoughts and feelings arising in my psyche … but where do they come from?

I know I exist … but I don't know *why* I exist.

I'm conscious of being alive … but I don't really know what life is.

I inhabit a vast universe … but I don't really know what the universe is.

I'm experiencing this moment … but I don't really know what this moment is.

Life is utterly mysterious, yet normally most of us go about our business as if being alive is nothing remarkable. We pretend we know what's going on, when really we don't. We act as if we understand what it is to be a human being, when actually it is an enormous enigma of mind-boggling proportions. As Albert Einstein, one of the greatest minds of all time, writes:

The human mind is not capable of grasping the universe.

I've spent my whole life wondering what life is. After five decades of passionate exploration, which has included some serious study and in-depth spiritual practice, an honest attempt at radical soul-searching and a monumental amount of philosophical chat, I've come to a fascinating conclusion.

What is life? *I don't know.*

I'm a pretty smart guy. I can read philosophical books and discuss quantum physics. But it seems to me that all my clever opinions float like flotsam on a vast sea of mystery. The edifice of information I've erected totters on the foundation of the ultimate enigma of existence … *that it is at all.*

The mystery of life is so enormous it leaves me speechless. It's not some riddle I will one day unravel, but real magic to be marvelled at. It's not a darkness my intellect can illuminate, but a dazzling radiance so splendid that my most brilliant ideas seem dull.

I invite you to really pay attention to the deep mystery with me right now and you'll feel your state of consciousness change.

Become intensely aware that you exist and how amazing that is.

See the familiar world with curious eyes.

Own up to how little you really understand reality.

Immerse yourself in wonder.

Albert Einstein enthuses:

> The most beautiful and deepest experience someone can have is the sense of the mysterious. It is the underlying principle of religion as well as all serious endeavour in art and science. He who can no longer pause to wonder and stand rapt in awe, is as good as dead; his eyes are closed.

THE MYSTERY AND THE STORY

Life is a mystery about which we tell stories. We all have a story about what life is, which we use to help us navigate our lives. A story that helps us understand what's going on. A story that gives us a sense of who we are. A story that gives life meaning. Our stories are wonderful. I love listening to people's stories. I'd love to hear your story.

We need a story to help us understand life. If we didn't have a story we'd be lost. The problem is that we can easily mistake the story for reality. We can invest so heavily in our beliefs about life that we forget that we really don't know what life is. We can become so caught up in our opinions that we miss the breathtaking mystery. And when this happens life becomes mundane and empty of wonder.

When I become embroiled with my story I find myself living in a sort of trance. I'm certain I know what's going on, even though I really don't. I exist in a state of numbness that I call normality and I feel only half alive. But when I wake up I can see that my story is a story. If I look deeper I discover that hidden behind my story is the pristine, virgin, untouchable mystery. And that's when I become deep awake.

If you want to awaken to the WOW you need to see through your story to the deep mystery. But please don't misunderstand me. I'm not suggesting you abandon your story. Having a story is essential and the more coherent it is the better. Philosophy can be seen as the art of creating a better story to live by.

If we didn't have a story we'd be lost and confused, rather than awake to the wonder of life. But it's not an either/or choice. We can approach things paralogically and be conscious of both the story and the mystery. We can see that on the surface of life our story helps us to understand our experience, but at the depths we really don't know what life is.

It amuses me how I can bob along on the surface of life, thinking I know what's going on, then suddenly remember the deep mystery. And when this happens everything changes, because my state of consciousness is profoundly transformed. I become deep awake … super-conscious … really alive. Then if I really immerse myself in the deep mystery I experience something extraordinary.

DEEP KNOWING

When I wonder about the unfathomable depths of life it feels as if I'm trying to formulate a primal question that is so enormous it's impossible to express. A question that is deeper than thought … something felt … something of the heart. Science offers many great insights into the nature of life that fascinate my mind, but it doesn't answer the inarticulate question of the heart. The books I read are full of valuable information, but words can't answer my wordless question.

It seems to me that all my ideas about life form a net of concepts that I cast into the ocean of mystery to catch the water. Yet when I immerse myself in the unfathomable enigma of existence the inarticulate question of the heart dissolves into the ocean of mystery. And I feel I've found the answer I'm looking for.

But this answer, like the question, is more of a feeling than a thought. I can't really express the inarticulate question, because it's too deep for words, and I can't really express the inarticulate answer, because it's also too deep for words.

When I see through all I think I know I experience the deep mystery. And when I go to the heart of the deep mystery I find myself experiencing a 'deep knowing' of something so immediate it can't be mediated by concepts, which transforms my experience of living. I feel a silent certainty that all is well. I feel an unshakable conviction in the essential goodness of life. I feel completely confident that what really matters is love. I don't know how I know … but *I know*.

It is one of the great paradoxes of awakening that not-knowing leads to deep knowing. As Robert Frost writes:

> We dance around in a ring, and suppose,
> But the Secret sits in the middle and knows.

CHAPTER 6

ENTERING

I want to share with you a simple meditation that can help you immerse yourself in the mystery of the moment, so that you can taste the deep awake state. I call this practice 'entering' because it was inspired by an old Zen story, which goes like this:

> A Zen master was out walking with one of his students who asked him: 'How can I awaken?'
>
> The master was quiet for a moment and then he replied: 'Can you hear that babbling brook? … *Enter there.*'

I love this story because in my imagination the student is looking for a clever spiritual teaching, but the master suggests that he can awaken by simply focusing his attention on the sound of the brook that has been babbling away in the background during their conversation. The master is telling him to become profoundly conscious of what he's already experiencing, by 'entering' into his sensual experience in the present moment.

I've found 'entering' my sensual experience to be a powerful way of awakening. When I enter into the immediacy of the senses they become a doorway to the deep awake state. Suddenly my everyday world, which may previously have seemed banal, is transformed into something mysterious and exquisite. My body becomes deeply relaxed. I feel sensually alive and intensely present.

Try it out now for yourself and I think you'll feel your state of consciousness shift immediately.

Stop and really listen to the sounds around you.

Then close your eyes and 'enter' the experience of listening for a while.

SENSUAL BREATHING

It is powerfully transformative to enter any of your senses, but I particularly enjoy entering the sensuality of breathing. Many spiritual traditions teach the practice of meditating on the breath, but it often sounds like a really dull thing to do. Actually, entering your breathing is a wonderfully sensual experience. In my twenties I spent a year sitting in meditation most of the time and what I discovered was that sinking my attention into my breath feels *really* good.

I'm going to describe how I experience entering my breath, then you can experiment with this practice and see how it is for you.

I am closing my eyes and becoming still.

I am noticing the feeling of my body sitting on this chair.

I am conscious of the air on my skin.

I am conscious of my breath as it rises and falls.

I am entering my breath by giving it my full attention.

I am conscious of the sensual flow of air in and out of my body.

I am sinking my attention into my breath and it's becoming intensely pleasurable to breathe.

The air feels thick and my body is starting to vibrate with energy.

My body is softening and it feels good to simply be.

I am dissolving into breathing.

I feel as if the universe is breathing me.

I am one with the sensation of breathing.

Simply to be here breathing is an utterly fulfilling experience.

I feel immersed in mystery.

I am in love with this moment just as it is.

I am in love with being.

WHAT STATE AM I IN?

When we find ourselves stuck in the superficial waking state, we simply need to enter the mystery of the moment and we will immediately begin the process of deep awakening. The tricky thing is noticing when we're only superficially awake, so that we can choose to become deep awake. When we're living in the semi-conscious state we call 'normal' it's hard to recognize how unconscious we are. And that's because we're largely unconscious. It's a paralogical Catch 22!

The secret is to develop the habit of noticing how awake you are. Instead of just paying attention to what's happening in your life story, you need to stop and ask yourself, 'What state of consciousness am I in?' This is like pinching yourself in a dream so that you wake up.

As you cultivate the habit of paying attention to your state you'll find yourself noticing when you're only superficially awake. Then you can choose to become deep awake. Here are some signs that you're only superficially awake.

If you're certain you know what's going on …
you're superficially awake.

If life seems banal and lacking in magic … you're superficially awake.

If you're so caught up in trying to get somewhere that you're ignoring being alive in the moment … you're superficially awake.

If you've become so serious that you can't laugh about life … you're superficially awake.

If you're missing the fact that your life is an astonishing adventure … you're superficially awake.

GUIDED MEDITATIONS

You can download audio versions of the guided meditations in this book from my website www.TimFreke.com

CHAPTER 7

THE DEEP I

We've made a start on our journey into the deep awake state. We've stopped being transfixed by the story that keeps us asleep in normal waking consciousness and become conscious of the deep mystery of life. Now we're ready to ask the great spiritual question, 'Who am I?'

When I ask myself this question the obvious response is, 'I am Tim.' Yet I'm not sure what that means. There are so many Tims. There's the Tim who is a philosopher writing this book. But he's quite different from the Tim who snuggles up in bed with his wife at the end of the day. Or the Tim who plays computer games with his children. Or the private Tim who no one else sees but Tim himself.

It amuses me that I even dress up in different clothes to clearly differentiate the different Tims. Shorts and a T-shirt for hanging out in the garden with the kids.

A sharp suit for public presentations. Jeans and a jacket for going to the school for parents' evening. Something more flamboyant for socializing with friends. The relief of no clothes at all for going to bed.

I have many different personas. The Greek word 'persona' means 'mask'. I wear many different masks. But who is underneath the mask? What happens if I perform a philosophical striptease and peel away all these passing identities? Who am I then? What is my naked self?

As I have studied my own nature over the years, I've discovered there are two paralogically opposite ways of seeing who I am. I can look at myself *objectively* and *subjectively*. How I answer the question, 'Who am I?' depends on which perspective I adopt. Let me take you through it.

The Objective Perspective

First I'm going to examine my objective identity.

Objectively I am a person in the world, who puts on different 'personas' to meet different situations.

Underneath all the roles I play and the clothes I wear I'm a naked body.

Objectively I am an *object* in the world.

The Subjective Perspective

Now I'm going to examine my subjective identity. Objectively what I am is easy to see, but subjectively what I am is less tangible.

> Subjectively I am the experiencer of this moment.

> I am the mysterious presence I call 'I'.

> I'm conscious of being the 'I' experiencing a stream of experiences right now.

> But what is the 'I'?

> The 'I' is aware of this moment, so I could describe the 'I' as 'awareness'.

> I am awareness witnessing an ever-changing flow of experiences that I call 'life'.

> Subjectively I'm a *subject* who is witnessing the world.

The Paradoxity of Identity

I have found that there are two paralogical poles to my identity.

> My objective identity is a body in the world.

My subjective identity is awareness that is experiencing my body in the world.

So am I a subject or an object? When I examine the reality of the moment I see that I am clearly both. Most of us find it easy to be conscious of being a body in the world, but find it harder to be conscious of being awareness. Spirituality encourages us to pay attention to the elusive subjective perspective. It urges us to 'look within' and become conscious of the deep I.

AN EXISTENTIAL RIDDLE

I want to share with you two of my favourite quotes that point to the deep I. The first comes from the Gnostic *Gospel of Thomas* and the second from the Hindu *Chandogya Upanishad*. I like putting these quotes together because, although they come from very different cultures, they're both saying exactly the same thing, which I find fascinating. In the first, Jesus announces:

I will reveal to you
what cannot be seen,
what cannot be heard,
what cannot be touched,
what cannot be thought.

What does this mean? The second quote makes things a bit clearer. It's in the form of a riddle:

> What is it that cannot be seen,
> but which makes seeing possible?
>
> What is it that cannot be heard,
> but which makes hearing possible?
>
> What is it that cannot be known,
> but which makes knowing possible?
>
> What is it that cannot be thought,
> but which makes thinking possible?

So … what is it that can't be seen or heard or touched or thought? It is awareness that is seeing and hearing and touching and thinking. It is the deep I that is conscious of all we experience. So here's my response to the riddle:

> Awareness experiences seeing,
> but has no colour or shape.
>
> Awareness experiences hearing,
> but makes no sound.
>
> Awareness experiences touching,
> but has no tangible form.

> Awareness experiences thinking,
> but is not a thought.

The great secret found at the heart of all the major spiritual traditions of the world is this. If you pay close attention to your identity, you will discover your subjective nature as awareness. This is your deep I. It is what the Hindu philosophers call the 'atman', the Buddhist masters call your 'buddha-nature', and the Christian mystics call your 'spirit'. The word 'spirit' means essence. The word 'essence' comes from the Latin *esse* meaning 'to be'. Your deep I is your *being*. It is what you *are*.

DEEP KNOWING THE DEEP I

We spiritually awaken by becoming conscious of our spiritual nature. We become deep awake by deep knowing the deep I. This can seem a tricky thing to do, so I'm going to describe how it is for me when I pay attention to the ineffable I of awareness.

> I can't see or hear or touch awareness, so it's extremely mysterious.

> I'm used to being conscious of what I'm experiencing, but the deep I is not something

I'm experiencing. It's the experiencer of all
I'm experiencing.

I'm used to paying attention to my unfolding
story, but the deep I isn't part of my story. It's the
presence of awareness witnessing the story.

I can't know the deep I as an object in my
experience, because the deep I is the subject.
I can only deep know the deep I by recognizing
my essential subjectivity.

I deep know the deep I by knowing the knower.

The deep I is ineffable, because it isn't something
I can see or hear or touch. Yet it is also obvious,
because it is my essential *being*.

A Blind Feeling of Being

Deep knowing the deep I can seem difficult, but
actually it simply requires you to pay attention to
something utterly obvious … you know that you exist.
A mystical Christian text called *The Cloud of Unknowing*
teaches that we need to become conscious of 'a naked
conception and a blind feeling of being'. Try it now and
I think you'll find your state of consciousness shifting.

Let go of your ideas about yourself and focus on a 'naked conception' of who you are.

Be conscious of a 'blind feeling of being'.

NAKED BODY AND NAKED BEING

My identity seems to be a complex of different personas that I adopt to play different roles in my life. But when I pay close attention I can see there is a simple paradoxity to my naked identity.

> Objectively, underneath all the clothes I wear to define my different personas, I am a naked body.

> Subjectively I am the presence of awareness, which is the constant background to all my experiences. This is my naked being.

As with all paradoxities these two opposite perspectives appear to be contradictory but are actually complementary.

> The body is what I *appear* to be.

> Awareness is what I *am*.

The Surface Self and the Deep I

I am going to explore the paradoxity of my identity in my experience right now and I invite you to explore the paradoxity of your identity with me.

> On the surface of my identity I appear to be a body called 'Tim'.

> At the depths of my identity I am awareness witnessing Tim's adventures.

> On the surface my body exists in the world of the senses.

> At the depths I am awareness, which can't be seen or heard or touched.

> On the surface I appear to be a physical object.

> At the depths I am essentially a spiritual subject.

CHAPTER 8

WHERE IS AWARENESS?

Objectively I'm a physical body. Subjectively I'm the presence of awareness. My body is sitting here in front of this computer. But where is awareness? If you looked into my eyes you'd connect with the presence of awareness, which would seem to be inside my head. But is that really true?

In my imagination I'm bending down in front of you so you can take a look. There's a big zip in my bald head, which I'm opening up so you can reach in and find awareness. You're searching with your hand in all the gooey porridge inside my head. And then you find it and pull it out to show the world … Tim's awareness … not as big as you might have expected!

It would be fun for that to happen. But it isn't going to, because awareness isn't inside my head. You can search about in my brain with a microscope, but you'll never find awareness. This is because awareness is not a thing in the world. It's not something we can see or hear or touch.

So where is awareness? Here's an interesting paralogical possibility to consider: awareness can't be found in the world because it's the other way round. The world exists in awareness. Awareness can't be found within my experience, because my experience is arising within awareness. Let me take you through it:

> Right now I am awareness experiencing a flow of thoughts and sensations.

> It's easy to understand that thoughts are arising within awareness, but it's equally true that sensations are arising within awareness as well.

> Everything I see, hear and touch is a sensation arising within awareness.

> I am listening to the sound of the wind blowing in the garden. This sound is arising within awareness. If it wasn't I wouldn't be conscious of it.

I am looking at a big pink poster of the artists Gilbert and George on my office wall. The colour is arising within awareness. If it wasn't I wouldn't be conscious of it.

I am enjoying the mellow flavour of the coffee I am drinking. The taste is arising within awareness. If it wasn't I wouldn't be conscious of it.

Everything I am experiencing is arising within awareness.

As a body I appear to exist within the world, but essentially I am awareness and the world exists within me.

The Spacious Presence of Awareness

One of the most profound teachings found at the mystical heart of all spiritual traditions is that essentially *you don't exist in the world.* Your deepest being can't be seen or heard or touched, because it has no form. The deep I is the formless presence of awareness within which all the forms of life are arising.

I invite you to play with this idea for a moment and see what happens:

Stop imagining that you are just the physical body you appear to be.

Instead imagine yourself to be a spacious presence within which your experience is arising.

When I first became open to this possibility I found it too subtle to hold on to for long, but as I have experimented with it I have found that it has profoundly transformed my experience of life. Now when I examine the present moment I can immediately see that both these paralogical statements are true:

There is an objective reality to my sense of being a physical body.

There is a subjective reality to my sense of being the spacious presence of awareness.

LUCID DREAMING AND LUCID LIVING

Many spiritual traditions compare life to a dream. I find this analogy really helps me understand the paradoxity of my identity. And it offers me a clear way of thinking about the deep awake state, because in my experience it is similar to 'lucid dreaming', except it happens when I am awake. Let me take you through it.

Usually when I dream at night I'm unconsciously engrossed in the dream. But sometimes I become conscious that I'm dreaming. This is called 'lucid dreaming'.

Something similar happens while I am awake. Often I'm unconsciously engrossed with my life story. But if I become deep awake I see that life is like a dream and I experience 'lucid living'.

When I dream lucidly I see the paradoxity of my identity. From one perspective I appear to be a character in my dream story. From another perspective I am the dreamer and I'm not *in* the dream at all.

When I live lucidly I see the paradoxity of my identity right now. From one perspective I appear to be a person within my life story. From another perspective I am spacious awareness witnessing all I am experiencing. I am not an object within my experience. I am the formless experiencer.

When I dream lucidly it is clear that awareness isn't inside the head of the character I appear to be in the dream. The dream is arising within awareness.

When I live lucidly it is clear that awareness isn't inside the head of the person I appear to be in the life story. My experiences are arising within awareness.

When I dream lucidly the dream continues as before, but my experience of dreaming is transformed, because I see that I am *both* in the dream *and* not in the dream.

When I live lucidly my life story continues as before, but my experience of living is transformed, because I see that I am *both* in the world *and* not in the world.

When I am deep awake and living lucidly I see life from a paralogical perspective and that brings real depth to my experience.

I am *both* engaged with the adventures of Tim *and* I know myself to be the spacious presence of awareness, within which the world is arising.

I see that in the life-dream I appear to be a separate individual, but my essential nature as awareness is one with life, just like a dreamer is one with a dream.

And when I know that I am one with life
I experience an intimate connectedness with
everything and everyone. I feel an all-embracing
love for life.

CHAPTER 9

PRESENCING

Nobel Prize-winning physicist Erwin Schrödinger arrived at conclusions that resonate with the insights of deep spirituality. He writes:

> We do not belong to this material world that science constructs for us. We are not in it; we are outside. We are only spectators. The reason we believe that we are in it, that we belong to the picture, is that our bodies are in the picture.

I'd like to suggest a simple practice I call 'presencing' which will help you become conscious of the deep I that is not in the world. This simply entails being conscious of yourself as awareness experiencing this moment. It involves knowing yourself to be the spacious presence within which all your experiences are arising like a dream.

Practices similar to presencing are important in many spiritual traditions. Zen master Yuansou says:

> All the various teachings and practices of Zen are only to encourage you to individually look back into yourself, so that you may know your essential nature and rest in a state of great peace and happiness.

Sound good? It's not as difficult as you might think. Becoming conscious of the deep I simply requires you to pay attention to your sense of *being,* which is actually obvious. As Padmasambhava, the founder of Tibetan Buddhism, explains so eloquently:

> It is your own awareness right now.
> It is simple, natural and clear.
>
> Why say, 'I don't understand what awareness is'?
> There is nothing to think about,
> just permanent awareness.
>
> Why say, 'I don't see the reality of awareness'?
> Awareness is the thinker of these thoughts.
>
> Why say, 'When I look I can't find it'?
> No looking is necessary.

Why say, 'Whatever I try doesn't work'?
It is enough to remain simple.

Why say, 'I can't achieve this'?
The void of pure awareness is naturally present.

Presencing This Moment

If you experiment with presencing I think you'll find
your state of consciousness shifting straight away.

Start by coming out of your normal waking state by
entering the delicious sensation of breathing and
immerse yourself in the mystery of the moment.

Then sink your attention into the depths of yourself
and become conscious of being the presence of
awareness witnessing all you are experiencing.

The Paradoxity of Attention

It is important to take a paralogical approach to
the practice of presencing. I'm not suggesting you
completely withdraw your attention from the world.
I am suggesting you can be conscious of *both* being the
spacious presence of awareness *and* being a person in
the world. I am suggesting you can live lucidly.

It may sound difficult to be conscious of both poles of your identity at once, but it becomes much easier if you understand the paralogical nature of your attention. To help you understand this I'd like you first to examine the paralogical nature of your eyesight, which is comparable.

> Examine your vision and you'll see that it focuses on a point around which you experience unfocused, peripheral vision.

Right now my vision is focused on the computer screen before me, but in my peripheral vision I can see the garden through the window, yet it's indistinct and out of focus. I am presuming you're experiencing something similar. Yes?

> Now examine your attention and you'll find that it also has a point of focus and a more diffuse, peripheral quality.

Right now my attention is focused on the words I'm writing, but in my peripheral attention I'm aware that it's getting late and I'll need to stop soon. I'm presuming that your attention is focused on reading this book. But in your peripheral attention you are conscious of whatever else is going on in your life right now.

The art of living lucidly is to move the focus of your attention between the surface of life and the depths, while retaining the other pole in your peripheral attention. This means that when you focus on the deep I, your surface self remains in your peripheral attention. And when you focus on your surface self, the deep I remains in your peripheral attention.

For me being deep awake is not about permanently focusing on the depths of life. It is shifting the focus of my attention in response to my life situations. For example, there is no greater joy I know than being immersed in the deep love that arises when I experience the big WOW of awakening. But this is not always appropriate. If I want to meet with my accountant the focus of my attention needs to be in the practical world, because when I'm swimming in love the whole idea of 'money' seems utterly absurd!

When I'm deep awake my attention is fluid not fixed, so I can respond to the changing demands of life. Sometimes I find myself dissolving into the ecstasy of the WOW and the story of Tim fades into the background. Sometimes I focus on Tim's challenges in life and the deep I is a quiet stillness that is present in the background. The focus of my attention flows between the paralogical poles.

At first it can be hard to do this. On my spiritual journey I initially found that while I was focused on Tim I forgot all about being awareness. But now I'm familiar with the deep awake state it's easier to keep the deep I in my peripheral attention when I'm focused on the story of Tim. Then I can return my focus to the depths of my being when I choose to. This means I can allow the focus of my attention to flow between the depths and the surface.

MY EXPERIENCE OF PRESENCING

I'm going to describe my experience when I focus my attention on being conscious of the deep I. Then I invite you to stop reading for a while and spend some time presencing your experience.

> I am conscious right now of an ever-changing stream of experiences.
>
> Normally I focus my attention on what I am experiencing, but I'm choosing to be conscious of myself as the *experiencer*.
>
> I am the experiencer of all that I'm experiencing.

I am the presence of awareness witnessing colours
… sounds … feelings … thoughts.

I am awareness that is looking, but can't be seen.

I am awareness that is listening, but can't be heard.

I am an unchanging stillness witnessing an
ever-changing flow of experiences.

I am conscious of being the formless presence of
awareness within which my experience is arising
like a dream.

CHAPTER 10

THE ONENESS OF BEING

At the mystical heart of deep spirituality is the profound idea that there is a primal oneness underlying the vast variety of life, so that although we appear to be individual *beings,* we are essentially all one *being.* You and I are like waves arising on a great ocean. On the surface we seem separate, but at the depths we are one.

Let's explore this amazing possibility:

You and I are distinct human bodies.

But essentially you are the formless presence of awareness … and so am I.

Without form separateness is impossible because there are no boundaries to discriminate anything as individual.

So the formless presence of awareness you experience as the deep I is not separate from the formless presence of awareness that I experience as the deep I.

At the depths of our being we are one.

The Dream of Brahman

The Hindu philosophers teach that the oneness of being, which they call Brahman, is a primal, formless awareness dreaming itself to be all the forms of life. The Zen masters say that everything is a thought arising within one 'big mind'.

In western spirituality the primal awareness is often called 'God'. But this mystical God is not a big person in heaven. God is the primal being dreaming itself to be all beings. You and I appear to be separate individuals, but essentially we are all God!

The Platonic philosophers teach that the primal *being* is in the process of *becoming* all that is. God is immanent in life. God is universal potentiality manifesting as the magnificence of the universe.

But God is not the *conscious* creator of
the universe.

God is *unconsciously* dreaming the world
into existence.

God is the *unconscious* primal awareness that
becomes *conscious* through the forms it dreams
itself to be.

Tim is experiencing the dream of life, but this
isn't Tim's dream. He is a character in the dream.

The unconscious primal awareness is dreaming
itself to be you and me as individual human
beings … and experiencing the dream of life
through us.

This is why you and I are experiencing different
perspectives on the same life-dream.

The Field of Unconscious Awareness

If you don't like the word 'God' we can explore the
same idea using the concept of a 'field', which is central
to physics. Scientists talk about fields such as the
'gravitational field' and the 'electromagnetic field',

which reach throughout the whole of space. We can use this concept for spiritual as well as scientific purposes.

Imagine an omnipresent, formless field of unconscious awareness, within which all the forms of life are arising.

Your body is an individual form arising within the primal field through which unconscious being becomes conscious of being.

Your body is a centre of conscious awareness illuminating a particular 'bubble' of experience within the field of unconscious awareness.

Conscious of Being the Unconscious Oneness

This understanding that the unconscious field of awareness arises as many centres of consciousness can help me describe my experience of oneness more clearly for you.

In the deep awake state I know I am the primal field that is arising as a particular centre of consciousness.

But this doesn't mean I'm conscious of what other centres of consciousness are experiencing.

Rather I am *conscious* of essentially being one with the field of *unconscious* awareness.

Let me take you through it:

Right now I am conscious of being the presence of awareness witnessing a unique stream of experiences.

If I pay attention to awareness, I am conscious that this formless presence has no qualities other than being, so has no boundaries to define it.

If I sink my attention deeply into the presence of awareness, it's like sinking down into the depths of the ocean of being.

The sense that I am an individual experiencing the world of separateness fades and I am immersed in a profound, undifferentiated oneness, beyond words to express.

On the surface I remain an individual conscious being. At my depths I am conscious of being the primal oneness of unconscious being.

The It-Perspective and the I-Perspective

Earlier in this book I suggested that science and spirituality should be seen as paralogically complementary perspectives on reality. I find it fascinating that both perspectives claim there is a primal oneness from which all the complex forms of life have arisen.

> This primal oneness can be viewed objectively *and* subjectively, giving us the complementary it-perspective and I-perspective.

> Science takes the it-perspective. It looks at things objectively and sees the primal oneness as energy that arises as matter, which becomes conscious through evolving into complex physical forms.

> Spirituality takes the I-perspective. It looks at things subjectively and sees the primal oneness as unconscious awareness, which becomes conscious through the forms it dreams itself to be.

> From both perspectives your individual being is one with the primal being, which is manifesting as all beings.

Erwin Schrödinger puts it beautifully when he writes:

> The individual I is an aspect of the whole, and
> identical to the universal I that projects itself
> as the world.

THE MYTH OF EVOLUTION

The great cosmological myth of our times is the scientific story of the evolving universe. It relates how the 'singularity' has birthed the vast variety of the universe, and become conscious through evolving into ever more complex forms, until it reaches the human form in which it is conscious of being.

Since ancient times spiritual myths have also explored the idea that the primal oneness of being is manifesting as the multiplicity of life, so that it can come to know itself. As the Gnostic sage Simon Magus stated 2,000 years ago in *The Great Announcement:*

> There is one power … begetting itself,
> increasing itself, seeking itself, finding itself …
> One root of the All.

In my imagination we're sitting together around a fire underneath a starry night sky, so that I can share with you my version of this myth. It may be a fantastical story but it resonates inside me like an ancient memory. It gives the human adventure the grandeur it deserves and helps me appreciate life in a deeper way. So come up close and I'll tell you an astonishing tale.

In the beginning was the wordless.

There was no one to think and nothing to think about.

The primal oneness of awareness was unconscious, because there were no experiences to be conscious of.

The oneness of awareness was like the presence of light without anything to illuminate, so paradoxically the light was dark.

But it is the nature of awareness to be aware, so within the primal awareness arose a great thought, which was the universe.

The timeless possibility for everything imagined the flow of time through which everything comes into being.

The oneness of being expressed its paralogical potentiality and appeared as the multiplicity of life.

The primal *being* manifested as the evolutionary process of *becoming*.

The oneness of unconscious awareness dreamed the story of life and progressively became more conscious through the evolving forms it imagined itself to be.

And so the primal oneness of unconscious being arose as many centres of conscious being.

So far so good … but this brings us to the twist that adds drama to our tale.

You see the primal awareness identified with each of the separate forms it appeared to be and didn't recognize its deeper identity as the oneness of being.

And here we are … that's you and me. Each one of us is the oneness of being believing itself to be just a separate individual.

This is not a satisfactory state of affairs, because when we're lost in separateness it's lonely and frightening.

We feel we're constantly missing something … and that's because we are.

Yet this underlying discontent pushes us to explore the depths of life.

We feel there must be more to existence, so we start to wonder.

This begins our journey of spiritual awakening.

At some point on this journey we become conscious of the deep I and we recognize that our essential being is one with the primal being.

And then … when we realize this … the primal being comes to know itself through us.

So the process of evolution is the primal oneness of unconscious being arising as separate centres of conscious being, so it can finally come to know that all is one.

The primal being is coming to self-knowledge by dreaming itself to be you and me on a journey of awakening to oneness.

Life is a journey from *unconscious oneness* through *conscious separateness* to *conscious oneness.*

And this huge realization brings us to the happy ending.

When we know that we are one with everything and everyone, we find ourselves in love with everything and everyone, because love is how oneness *feels*.

When we're conscious of the oneness of being, we fall in love with all beings.

We simply love *being*.

So our epic fable turns out to be a love story … and that's what makes it worth telling.

CHAPTER 11

DEEP AWAKE MEDITATION

I want to invite you to explore the depths of your being by experimenting with deep awake meditation. This is similar to presencing except it involves withdrawing your attention from the world and dissolving it into the oneness of being.

The word 'meditation' comes with a certain amount of baggage. It can sound like a serious spiritual endeavour, in which we earnestly try to become more awake. But I don't approach meditation in this way. I meditate because it is a wonderful thing to do. Viewing meditation as a spiritual 'discipline' makes it feel like something I'm confined by, when it's actually something that sets me free. I encourage you to practise for the pleasure of it. Don't make meditation a self-righteous chore! As spiritual philosopher Alan Watts explains:

> We could say that meditation doesn't have a reason or doesn't have a purpose. In this respect it's unlike almost all other things we do except perhaps making music and dancing. When we make music we don't do it in order to reach a certain point, such as the end of the composition. If that were the purpose of music then obviously the fastest players would be the best.

> Also, when we are dancing we are not aiming to arrive at a particular place on the floor as in a journey. When we dance, the journey itself is the point, as when we play music the playing itself is the point. And exactly the same thing is true in meditation. Meditation is the discovery that the point of life is always arrived at in the immediate moment.

DEEP ASLEEP AND DEEP AWAKE

To help you understand what happens in deep meditation I want to explore the paralogical relationship between the deep awake state and the deep asleep state.

> The oneness of being can be seen as formless unconscious awareness, which becomes conscious through the forms it dreams itself to be.

> I am the primal oneness of awareness conscious through Tim.

> When I fall deep asleep at night my experience of myself as a centre of consciousness dissolves back into the primal field of unconscious awareness.

> In the deep asleep state I have no objective or subjective identity. There's no self … no other … no time. I exist but I'm not conscious that I exist.

> I *unconsciously* dissolve into the primal oneness by falling deep asleep.

> Meditation allows me to *consciously* dissolve into the primal oneness and become deep awake.

> When I wake up in the morning I occasionally experience a blissful afterglow from the deep asleep state, which is a glimpse of how good it feels to be immersed in the deep oneness.

When I meditate I allow myself to *consciously* bathe in the blissful ocean of being.

MEDITATION AND THE MIND

It is often presumed that meditation is about stopping thinking, but I feel this is a mistake. When I meditate my thoughts come and go, but I don't fight them. I simply become conscious that I'm listening to myself talking to myself. I pay attention to the silent presence of awareness that is listening.

In the same way that a puddle of water becomes transparent if you stop splashing in it and let the mud settle, so my thoughts become less agitated when I stop focusing my attention on them. Then my mind naturally becomes calm, which means I can easily sink into the deep awake state.

I've spent long periods of my life exploring meditation so I'm often able to dive straight into the depths of my being. But this isn't always the case. If I pay too much attention to my thoughts I find myself floating off into a dream. I used to regard a dreamy meditation as a 'bad' meditation. These days I simply focus on what this experience can teach me.

As I dream off I examine how it feels to be sucked into a semi-conscious state. Sometimes it can be an effort to resist the inertia of falling asleep. It feels as if I have to extricate myself from a viscous stickiness and pull myself back to a more conscious state.

What fascinates me about this experience is that something similar happens in my everyday life. I often get sucked into my story when I'm awake. And it feels as if my story is sticky, so it's hard to extricate myself. There is the dead weight of inertia pulling me into unconsciousness, which it takes an effort of will to resist.

This means that when I start to dream off in meditation, I no longer see it as some sort of spiritual failure. I see it as a wonderful opportunity to build the psychological 'muscles' that allow me to become more awake in my daily life.

Being deep awake is effortless, but waking up can take psychological effort. If you'd like to get a visceral understanding of this, simply lie down on the floor and then get up. Even if you're very fit you'll find you need to make some effort to get to your feet, but once you're up it's effortless. It's similar with spiritual awakening.

MY EXPERIENCE OF MEDITATION

For me meditation is an opportunity to take time off from the pressures of living and dissolve into the vast expanses of my deepest being. I appreciate whatever I experience in meditation. Sometimes there's simply a sense of stillness and peace. Other times meditation is so wonderful I find it very hard to put into words … but I'm going to give it a go:

> When I practise deep awake meditation
> I understand why the Hindus talk about the
> primordial vibration of 'om', because I feel as
> if I'm merging with a low vibration that underlies
> all that is. I am consumed by ommmmmmm …

> I understand why the Gnostics talk about the
> *pleroma,* or 'fullness', because I feel as if I'm
> dissolving in a vast emptiness that is effervescent
> with vitality.

> I understand why the Gnostics describe the oneness
> of being as a 'dazzling darkness', because the
> emptiness seems to be sparkling with 'dark light'.

> I understand what people mean by the
> 'sound of the silence', because the silence
> has the sound of a million miniscule tinkling
> bells, and I feel submerged by waves of ringing,
> which are rising and falling in the void.

I understand what the devotional mystics mean by loving God as the divine Beloved, because I find myself falling in love with the primal being that is the source of all.

When I reach within it feels as if God is reaching out to welcome me. I feel as if I am relaxing into the arms of the great Beloved … as if we're lovers who've been longing to be together … to caress each other … to be one with each other.

I feel one with the one I love … the oneness that I love … the one 'I' which *is* love.

DISSOLVING INTO DEEP BEING

I'm going to remember my meditation yesterday as if it was happening now and share the experience with you. Then I encourage you to take some time to experiment with deep awake meditation for yourself.

I've retreated into the quiet of my bedroom where I won't be disturbed.

I am making my body comfortable.

I am becoming relaxed and alert.

I am conscious of the room around me and the sounds outside the window.

I am conscious of what a wonder life is and how mysterious it is to be alive.

I close my eyes and let go of my story.

I am intensely conscious of the present moment.

I enter the delicious sensation of breathing.

As I do this my body begins to soften and my mind begins to calm.

I am entering the beautiful textures of my breath … the cool air coming into my body and the warm air leaving my body.

I am spacious awareness presencing breathing.

Now I am turning my attention deeply within.

It feels as if I am sinking further and further back into the depths of my being.

I am dissolving my attention into the primal ground from which my conscious attention is arising.

I am immersed in the primordial vibration of the dazzling darkness.

The stillness is full of ommmmmmm.

The emptiness is alive with presence.

There's an oceanic feeling of oneness.

I feel as if I'm melting into an ocean of bliss.

I am enfolded within the safe arms of the Beloved.

All is one in boundless love.

CHAPTER 12

DEEP LOVE

In the deep awake state I experience the oneness of being as an all-embracing love. This is beautifully expressed using religious language in the *First Letter of John,* which declares:

> God is love
> and those that live in love
> live in God
> and God lives in them.

For me God is the oneness of being that is arising as all beings. And when I know God I experience a love that embraces all beings.

Religious traditions often portray God as the lord of the universe who decrees how we should live in holy books, which are the 'word of God'. But God doesn't speak to us. God is the primal silence that speaks *through* us. All words are human words and conditioned by the human experience of living in time. They are at best partial expressions of a truth that can never be articulated. There is no 'word of God', but if there were it would be only one word. And that word is 'love'.

Devotional Love

During the early years of my awakening I experienced an intense love affair with God, full of passionate longing when we felt apart and deep communion when we found each other again. It is such a precious feeling when, as the Christian mystic Hildegard of Bingen puts it, 'the mystery of God hugs you in its all-encompassing arms'.

Many spiritual traditions describe spiritual awakening as leading to an experience of intense devotion to God. Other traditions maintain that having a devotional relationship with God characterizes a lesser awakening. It shows we're still enmeshed in the illusion of separateness, because in reality we are one with God.

In my experience these two approaches are complementary not contradictory. Being one with God and being in love with God are paralogically different ways of experiencing the same awakened state. When I'm deep awake I see I am *both* separate *and* not separate from all that is. I am one with the primal being *and* I'm this separate individual called 'Tim' who feels intense love for the primal being.

Loving Being

The great Christian mystic, Meister Eckhart, teaches that 'God is being' and urges us to 'love God'. When I first read this it occurred to me that if 'God is being' then to 'love God' is to love *being*. It is to love *being* here and now as Tim. It is to love the *being* of everything and everyone. It is to love all that is, simply because it is.

When I love being it feels good to be. I know how much I want to exist. This love of being is something that permeates the whole of nature. Biologists call it the 'survival instinct', but it is much more than just the will to survive. It's an experience of the fundamental joy of living.

It seems to me that this love of being is always present, even when I'm not conscious of it. Whenever I enter the deep awake state there's an unconditional, all-embracing love of being, waiting to welcome me with open arms.

Loving the Nature of Things

When I'm deep awake I find myself in love with *both* the oneness of being *and* the exquisite world of appearances. I become awed by the beauty of the world. I become overcome with wonder at the multifarious richness of life. I see the numinous in nature. The mystical theologian Rudolf Otto describes the feeling of communing with the natural world as:

> The sense of being immersed in the oneness of nature, so that man feels all the individuality, all the peculiarities of natural things in himself. He dances with the motes of dust and radiates with the sun; he rises with the dawn, surges with the wave, is fragrant with the rose, rapt with the nightingale: he knows and is all being, all strength, all joy, all desire, all pain in all things inseparably.

In mythological language when we fall in love with the nature of things we're paying homage to the divine Goddess. She represents the mysterious appearances of life, just as God represents the mysterious essence of life. God is the life-dreamer. She is the life-dream. She is everything we can see and hear and touch and taste. She is Mother Nature. We are living in her sacred presence right now. My deep love affair is with *both* God as the mysterious ground of being *and* Goddess as all the wonderful qualities of being.

In the Gnostic *Gospel of Thomas* Jesus proclaims:

> The kingdom of heaven is laid out upon the earth, but people don't see it.

In my experience when I'm superficially awake the world can seem familiar and dull. But when I'm deep awake the world becomes a lucent miracle shimmering with mystery. I see that heaven is truly here on earth.

THE SPECTRUM OF LOVE

Deep love is not some ethereal experience. It's a tangible love I feel in my body. Yet deep love is much more than just a great feeling. It's a total relationship with reality. When I'm deep awake I feel deep love flowing out from the depths of my being into my heart to make me tender, into my mind to make me wise, into my body as sensual aliveness, and out into the world as compassionate action.

Deep love includes the whole spectrum of love, from sublime love of being, devotion to God, communion with nature … to human affection for a friend, romantic love of a partner, the instinctual love of a child, the erotic love of sexual intimacy, the sensual love of pleasure, the engaged love of enjoying what we do. Some spiritual traditions teach that our human loves are lesser loves, which we must be willing to sacrifice if we want to experience the divine love of God. But it seems to me this is a terrible error born of either/or thinking.

The love I feel for my children is not inferior to my love of God. It's a personal expression of the one love that contains all love within it. Deep love is a primal love that arises in my life as all my personal loves. Deep love embraces and completes all my personal loves.

From animal sex to transcendental devotion, love is the experience of the two becoming one while remaining two. When we love we feel we are separate and not separate from each other. And both are important because love is the experience of communing as one, which can only arise because we are two.

Alan Watts evocatively describes his experience of awakening to love:

> All at once it became obvious that the whole thing was love-play, where love means everything that the word can mean, a spectrum ranging from the

red of erotic delight, through the green of human endearment, to the violet of divine charity, from Freud's libido to Dante's 'love that moves the sun and stars'. All were so many colours issuing from a single white light.

THE HOLE IN THE SOUL

When I'm spiritually asleep there's always a feeling that something is missing. There's a hole in my soul that I don't know how to fill. I try to change my life so that things feel right, but nothing works. If I really pay attention, however, it becomes obvious that I'm longing for love. Without love my life is empty and meaningless.

The Buddha taught that the unawakened life is permeated by a type of suffering he called *dukkha*. This is an underlying unease and discontent. An existential SOS that arises from the knowledge of death. A fundamental sense of separateness from others. An alienation from the world.

The Gnostic Christians wrote about this debilitating alienation in texts such as *Allogenes,* which means 'the stranger'. And this message resonates down the ages into the French writer Albert Camus's existentialist novel *L'Étranger,* the title of which also translates as 'the stranger'. When we're lost in separateness we feel like a stranger in a strange land.

This perpetual sense of discomfort and alienation is hard to avoid because it arises from the fact that we are conscious individuals. To be conscious is to be separated from life as a solitary observer of the world. To feel our human vulnerability is inevitably distressing.

We seek to alleviate this distress by making ourselves physically and financially secure. But we're never secure enough to withstand the storms of life. We seek to alleviate this distress by becoming important and respected. But we're never important enough to be overlooked by death. We seek to alleviate this distress by becoming successful and admired. But the emptiness within makes all our triumphs seem hollow. And then as the Indian poet Kabir says:

> Everything we do has some strange sense of failure in it.

Deep down most of us know that only love can fill the hole in the soul. Only love can set us free from the debilitating *dukkha* that lurks in the shadows on even our sunniest days. Only love can truly mitigate all that is bad in life and allow us to truly celebrate all that is good.

We all crave love as if it's rare and hard to find, but there is no shortage of love if we look within to the source of love. The truth is we live and breathe and have our being in an ocean of love. And when we understand this we can smile wryly at the irony of the human condition with wise Kabir who writes:

> I laugh when I hear that the fish in the water
> is thirsty.

Longing for Love

The hole in the soul is disturbing but it's also a blessing, because it demands that we fill it. When our superficial attempts to fill the inner emptiness fail, we start to look deeper and become spiritual seekers. And when we spiritually awaken we find ourselves immersed in deep love. Then we know that this love is what we've been longing for all along.

In my experience this longing to feel deep love has become a passionate desire to keep on waking up and going deeper. It is the fuel that keeps me going through the challenges of the spiritual journey. It is missing the Beloved when we're apart and yearning to be reunited with all my heart. It is aching to awaken.

I have found that when I really want to wake up, I start to wake up. When I really yearn for deep love, deep love reaches out to me. When my deepest desire is to be immersed in the mystery, the mystery welcomes me in. In one of Kabir's poems God declares:

> When you *really* look for me,
> You will see me instantly.

On my *Deep Awakening* retreats I offer people a powerful experience of deep love, so when they return home they can remember how good it feels. This means that when they feel the hole in the soul, they can recall the deep awake state and feel motivated to find it again, because they know they're really longing for love.

The deeper we go into the awakened state, and the more frequently we return to it, the easier it becomes to remember how much we long to wake up when we've fallen asleep. If we recall times when we've been in love with life, we naturally feel the desire to become more conscious again. And it's the sincerity of this longing that will lead us back home to the deep awake state.

The Magic That Makes Life Sweet

For me it's love that makes life worth living. When people come on my retreats it's my sincere aspiration that everyone experiences the natural wonder of deep love … and the vast majority do. As we melt into love we take each other deeper into the WOW, and there's no mistaking how this *feels,* because the love vibrates in every cell of the body. The divisions dissolve and we relax into the naturalness of playing together in the blissful ocean of being.

From my first awakening to this present moment my ideas have changed and matured, but the conviction that life is ultimately all about love has remained. I call myself a philosopher because I adore good ideas. But that's just a cover story to get people to take me seriously. Really I'm a love junkie.

I admitted this recently at the end of a retreat and a wonderful woman called out, 'You're not a love junkie … you're a dealer!' That's one of the nicest compliments I've ever had. It's funny because it's true. So here's what I'm really saying in this book:

> Hey! Are you looking for some deep love to fill the hole in your soul? I've got the real deal here and it's going for free. This is the magic that makes life sweet. This is the big WOW you've been waiting for. And when you taste it once you'll be hooked for life.

CHAPTER 13

I TO I MEDITATION

It's wonderful when we share the awakened state with others, because it amplifies the experience of deep love. During my *Deep Awakening* retreats I guide people through a variety of 'I to I meditations', which involve connecting with a partner through the senses and experiencing a profound communion at the depths of our shared being.

As I've developed and experimented with these practices the results have astonished me. They are by far the most transformative practices I've ever experienced. I invite you to join me at one of my retreats, so you can experience for yourself how totally amazing it feels to commune deeply with a large group of people.

For now I'm going to share with you one simple I to I meditation that you can easily practise with a friend. When I guide this meditation at my retreats I play soft music to help us relax. Here's what you and your partner need to do:

Sit in front of each other and gaze into each other's eyes.

Be conscious that you're looking at a beautiful face, but also be conscious that what you are really connecting with is much deeper than that.

You are connecting deep I to deep I.

You are connecting with awareness looking back at you … but you can't see awareness.

You are the presence of awareness, which is looking but can't be seen, connecting with the presence of awareness, which is looking but can't be seen.

Go deeper still and become conscious of the oneness of being.

You are the oneness connecting with itself by appearing as two.

Sit with that beautiful paradox and see how it feels.

Safe Intimacy

When practising I to I gazing it's extremely important to feel safe. We habitually look from the perspective of the separate self, so when we gaze into another person's eyes we may fear it is intrusive, but it isn't. No one has access to our secret thoughts and feelings. These remain private and that's how it should be.

I to I gazing is about seeing through the personal self to the impersonal oneness. This practice won't help us get to know each other *personally,* which takes lots of shared experiences over time. But getting to know each other on this deep level takes no time at all. It happens the moment we look through the separate self to the deep I.

I See You

In the movie *Avatar* the characters greet each other with the phrase 'I see you'. That's how it feels when I do this meditation, because I really see the other person and I feel really seen. Then as we commune with each other there is a silent knowing that at the depths of our being we are one.

In India people use the greeting 'namaste', which can be understood as meaning 'I acknowledge you from the place in me where you and I are one'. This I to I meditation enables us to acknowledge to each other that we are essentially one. And when this happens it's WOW.

In the Hindu tradition meeting with a spiritual master is regarded as a great blessing, because we find ourselves resonating with the master's awakened state of consciousness, which transforms our own state. This is known as *darshan*. In my experience when we connect deeply we can feel the joy of *darshan* with anyone, because actually we're all great spiritual beings. Walt Whitman describes how this feels when he writes:

> In the faces of men and women I see God, and in my own face in the glass.

Beautiful Otherness

When I practise I to I gazing to connect with another person, I see how wonderful it is that we're separate *and* not separate, because it is being *both* that allows us to commune in love. I find myself falling in love with my partner's gorgeous individuality. I see that what makes them so special is that they're different from me. I appreciate their unique qualities of being as a beautiful expression of the oneness of being. In the lyrics of the electronica band Bent:

Beautiful otherness
Love you because of this
Lost in the loveliness
Of your beautiful otherness

Connecting I to I in Everyday Life

What's so great about I to I gazing is that it simply involves looking, which is what we're already doing all the time. This means we can use this practice to transform our relationships with others in our everyday lives.

When I'm with someone our eyes often meet. What I experience depends on my state of consciousness. If I'm deep awake I see through the separate self to the deep I that can't be seen … and there's a moment of deep connection.

States of consciousness are catching, because we resonate together. So when I connect deeply with someone, they often begin to wake up. And I like to think that they then go on to connect more deeply with other people that they meet, who may also be touched by the experience. So a ripple of awakening spreads out into the world.

I TO I GAZING

In my imagination I'm going to recall the last time
I practised I to I gazing and describe what happened.
Then I encourage you to try this with a friend when
the time is right.

> My partner and I are sitting opposite each other
> with our eyes closed.

> We are entering and presencing the moment in
> the deep awake state.

> When we feel ready we open our eyes and gently
> gaze at each other.

> First I'm conscious of what I can see … colours and
> shapes that make up the image of a beautiful face.

> I focus on my partner's eyes and I know that I am
> connecting with another human being, full of hopes
> and fears, memories and dreams, just like me.

> My partner's face is etched with their experiences
> of life, but their eyes are strangely ageless.

> It feels as if I am looking through the mature adult
> to see my partner as an innocent child.

I am looking through the surface self to the deep I.

I am awareness that cannot be seen … connecting through looking … with awareness that cannot be seen.

I am the oneness of being arising as Tim looking at the oneness of being arising as my partner.

My partner's face seems luminous and beautiful.

Sometimes it feels as if when I look through one eye I am connecting with the individual self and when I look through the other eye I am connecting with universal being.

How delightful!

We are communing as one and two … separate and not-separate … the same and different.

We are dissolving into each other.

We are in love with each other.

CHAPTER 14

THE EGO AS HERO

We started our journey together in the mystery of
the moment looking for the deepest answer to the
question 'Who am I?' and we've become conscious of
the paradoxity of identity. We've discovered that you
and I are the oneness of being appearing as particular
human beings. And we've seen that when we embrace
both poles of our identity we can commune with each
other in love.

Many spiritual traditions, however, take an
either/or approach to the paradoxity of identity. They
teach that we need to reject our human individuality
if we want to experience the oneness of being. The
separate self is seen as an obstacle to our awakening
and often derogatively referred to as the 'ego'.

In my experience, however, we don't need to eradicate the separate self to awaken to oneness. When I'm deep awake 'Tim' doesn't disappear in a puff of spiritual enlightenment. On the contrary, Tim comes to life. I find myself cherishing my individuality and appreciating the poignant beauty of the personal life. So I have come to question the ubiquitous idea of the evil ego. Indeed I want to suggest that nurturing a healthy ego is necessary and desirable.

There's a little game I play when I want to check out if a spiritual teaching really makes sense. I ask myself if I would share the idea with my children. If the answer is 'no' then I usually find there's something missing from the teaching. So I want to ask this: would I tell my daughter not to develop an ego?

The answer is obvious to me. No, I wouldn't. I want her to grow up with a clear sense of herself as a distinct individual. I want her to become a strong, independent woman who knows who she is, so she can draw boundaries when necessary. And this is because possessing a robust ego is a blessing not a curse.

When I started speaking about spiritual awakening I used to emphasize the wonder of oneness, because people seemed stuck in separateness. These days I find myself emphasizing the importance of separateness, because I meet too many people who view their individuality as a problem to be overcome. This makes them dismiss the miracle of human life as a meaningless illusion, which cuts them off from the experience of deep love.

Vilifying the ego as a spiritual enemy doesn't help us awaken. It merely encourages us to wage an internal civil war against ourselves, which we can only lose. We've spent our lives cultivating our personal identity, imperfect as it is. Are we really now to conclude this was all a big mistake? Surely that would be perverse.

Celebrating the Separate Self

In this book we've explored how all individual beings are expressions of the oneness of being, but this doesn't mean that individuality is an irrelevant illusion. There is a reality to the separate self and the world of multiplicity, just as much as there is a reality to the oneness of being in which there is no separateness. They are paralogically complementary perspectives on reality.

The separate self is a prerequisite for awakening, not an obstacle to be overcome. You and I are separate centres of conscious being within the unconscious oneness of being. If this were not the case we wouldn't be conscious at all … let alone spiritually awakened.

People often come to my retreats because, although they understand that all is one, they find it hard to actually experience the reality of oneness. This is sometimes because they're stuck in an either/or approach to spiritual awakening. They're convinced that they will never awaken to oneness as long as they experience themselves as an individual ego. They're waiting for the separate self to disappear, but it just won't go … and it's not going to!

Trying to eradicate the ego is like trying to have 'left' but no 'right'. No matter how far left we go, we can't get rid of right, which just keeps following us! Attempting to get rid of the ego is attempting to have one pole of a paradoxity without the other. This is impossible, so we continually fail. And while we're busy failing to experience the oneness of being *instead of* the separate self, we don't see how easy it is to be conscious of the oneness of being *as well as* the separate self.

Of course when we are identified with *just* the separate self we can become 'egotistical', in the sense of the word that implies we are selfish, self-obsessed and narcissistic. I'm not saying that's a good thing. I simply want to suggest that our humanity is essentially something to celebrate not denigrate. And that as we awaken to deep love the separate self becomes a vehicle to express that love.

According to the modern scientific story of evolution the universe has been working towards manifesting the possibility of individual conscious beings for more than 13 billion years. Has that all been some enormous waste of time? Surely individuality is not some pernicious delusion, but rather the greatest achievement in the evolution of life?

Awakening Requires Individuality

I want to suggest that far from being a problem the personal self is the foundation from which we can spiritually awaken. Our individuality is a gloriously particular expression of the infinite potentiality of being, through which the primal oneness can experience life.

As we mature we all struggle to individualize ourselves as a particular person. We become conscious of the world by picking up a picture of what reality is from those around us. We're conditioned by our culture. At this stage we exhibit the beginnings of individuality, but we're still largely unconscious. We really start to become individuals when we learn to question our conditioning.

When we doubt the received wisdom of our culture, we separate ourselves from the unconscious herd. This makes us different and can be isolating. But it's a necessary step on the path of awakening. If we are to experience life in a deeper way, we need to think for ourselves and see through the 'common nonsense' generally taken for granted.

So it seems to me that we become more conscious by becoming more individual not less. Eventually through the process of becoming a distinct individual we can become conscious enough to spiritually awaken. Then we become conscious of the paradoxity of our identity, so we realize that on the surface we appear to be separate, but at the depths all is one.

NON-DUALITY AND NO DOER

Over the last 20 years I've watched 'non-dual' spirituality become more and more popular. I was part of this process in the early days because I was delighted that people were waking up to oneness. But I soon became concerned that they were being left confused in a cold, empty world, devoid of meaning.

Modern non-dual spirituality is often characterized by a complete denial of the reality of the individual self.

A central claim is that awakening requires the understanding that there is 'no doer' with free will to choose and act. The idea of an individual agent with volition arises from the illusion of separateness. In reality everything is just happening, and seeing this leads to the realization of 'no self', which is the 'final truth'.

From one perspective I agree that everything is arising spontaneously as one, and when I first experienced this deep realization it was truly astonishing. All is the one flow of life. The writing of these words is happening as part of that one flow just as naturally as the sun rises each morning. On a deep level the oneness of awareness is *doing* everything, just as the dreamer is *doing* everything in a dream.

But that's only one side of the paradoxity. From the other perspective Tim's experience of free choice is very important indeed. The primal being is *unconsciously* dreaming up the world, but it is *conscious* through Tim. This means that the *unconscious* oneness of being can *consciously choose* to do this or that through Tim.

It is often claimed by non-dualists that there is no free will because consciousness is a passive presence that merely witnesses the world. But in passively witnessing the world consciousness changes the world. When the oneness of being witnesses the world through Tim this can lead to a thought arising from the depths … 'I think I'll do this' … and that initiates action.

It's taken billions of years of evolution to get us to the place where the primal being can make conscious choices through us. Most of evolution has been unconscious and therefore pretty haphazard. But now the primal being can consciously think about what it's going to do. And it's doing that through you and me!

I am often told by non-dualists that 'Tim' is no more than a puppet whose autonomy is an illusion. But I suggest this confuses two paralogical perspectives. From one perspective all is one and everything is just happening, so there's no separate 'Tim' to be a puppet or have volition. From the other perspective everything is separate and I exist as a person called 'Tim', who can clearly choose how he reacts to life. This is one of his defining qualities as a human being.

It seems to me that our experience of choice is a reality it is absurd to deny. In fact our freedom is much more extensive than we normally acknowledge. We are free in this moment to do innumerable things. Our freedom is overwhelming. Indeed it seems to me that if we could allow ourselves to be as free as we truly are, we'd make much better choices in our lives, and be much happier. All it takes is for us to become more conscious. Because the more conscious we are the more freedom of choice we experience.

THE PATHOLOGY OF DEPERSONALIZATION

We need a secure sense of our individuality if we are to awaken to the oneness of being. When this is not present the process of awakening becomes transformed into a pathology. For psychologists the condition of 'depersonalization' is a type of mental illness associated with extreme anxiety, not a higher state of consciousness.

People suffering from depersonalization feel that they have lost their sense of self. They describe living 'outside of the body' as 'an observer' who is 'detached from life'. They experience what psychologists call 'derealization', which is the experience that 'life is like a dream'. It sounds uncannily similar to the experience of awakening. But people suffering from this condition don't wake up to deep love. They find the experience of depersonalization extremely distressing.

There's someone I know well who has been suffering from depersonalization, which has made him very anxious. The irony for me is that while I've been writing this book about awakening, he's been reporting many similar experiences to those I've been describing. Except for him they're extremely negative.

Although he's not familiar with my philosophical ideas, he's been telling me that 'life seems like a dream' … 'I don't feel like I am a person' … 'I feel like a disembodied observer' … 'I can't stop paying attention to my breath'. And he's been hating all of this. So I haven't been advising him to dive deeply into the experience and spiritually awaken. I've been doing the opposite. I've been trying to ground him in his separate self so the depersonalization passes, which is gradually happening.

First we need a robust sense of being a separate individual. When this is strong enough it can support a conscious awakening to our deeper being. When a strong separate self is absent, the natural process of awakening is transformed into the pathology of depersonalization. Many ancient spiritual traditions understood this, which is why they reserved the deep teachings of oneness for those who had reached a mature age and possessed a robust individual ego.

THE HERO OF THE STORY

It seems to me that the ego is the hero not the villain of the spiritual adventure. The ego is the surface self through which the deep I can experience the adventure of living. The ego is a character in the dream of life around which the life-dreamer weaves a cracking tale.

If I look at my own experience Tim is clearly the hero of the life story. He's the star of the show. Other people come and go, but Tim is in every scene. His wife, Debbie, plays romantic love interest. His best mate, Pete, plays comic sidekick. There's a whole load of extras who figure now and then. But Tim's the main man.

The paradoxity of life means that as a conscious individual each one of us is the hero of the story of life. Looked at from one perspective we appear to be irrelevant specks of dust in a vast universe, who are here for a moment and then gone. But from another perspective everyone is the centre around which the universe revolves. How wonderful!

When I understand that I am *both* an irrelevant speck *and* the star of the show, it makes me feel *both* humble *and* empowered. I want to encourage you *both* to be conscious of the oneness of being *and* to feel empowered as a unique individual who is the hero of your amazing life adventure.

A Work in Progress

Please don't misunderstand me. When I portray the ego in a positive light, I'm not pretending that being a person isn't a mixed blessing. Who doesn't look at themselves and find parts of their personality they wish weren't there? But this doesn't mean our individuality is somehow intrinsically bad.

My own experience of being Tim has been a grand adventure, but his unconsciousness has often filled me with despair and shame. Yet I don't see Tim as a spiritual burden, because I've come to love him despite his flaws. He can be difficult to live with, but I've become patient with that. I don't want to eradicate the ego I've struggled to develop as I've become a distinct individual. I want to appreciate the ego as the protagonist at the centre of the story of my life.

The Sufis encourage us to see the individual self as a work of art that we're in the process of creating. I like this idea. Tim is a work of art that I'll refine and rework until my dying day. He's imperfect, of course, which is tough on everyone. But it's only to be expected. He's a work in progress. He's an attempt at a conscious, loving human being. For as Carl Jung says:

Every human being is an attempt at a human being … a throw from the depths.

CHAPTER 15

LOVING BEING HUMAN

Many spiritual traditions teach that if we want to awaken to our essential divinity we need to suppress our troublesome humanity. We need to eradicate our passions. Fear, anger and desire are particularly deplorable. Lust is really bad. Our attachments are a problem, too.

Such attitudes are so common in spiritual circles that I once took them seriously, but not anymore. Once again it seems to me that such teachings actually make it harder to awaken, because we believe there are things about our nature that we must overcome, when actually all we need to do is notice our deeper identity *as well*.

I used to believe that if I was awake enough I'd become an enlightened über-being who was no longer troubled by disturbing emotions and passions. But actually I've remained as human as ever. And I'm pleased about that, because I no longer want to be superhuman. I've fallen in love with being human.

For me the wonderful thing about awakening is that it enables me to embrace my human nature just as it is. So in this chapter I want to explore a paralogical approach to our passions, which sees them as both good and bad. I want to articulate a way of awakening that embraces our ambiguous humanity as well as our deep divinity. Let's start with that great bogeyman 'fear'.

Safe Vulnerability

Being human can be pretty scary, don't you think? We're so small and fragile in such a dangerous world. Suffering is a reality we can't avoid. Old age wears the body away. Death is waiting to surprise us at any moment. It seems to me that if we're not frightened by the human predicament we simply haven't been paying attention!

Some spiritual traditions teach that fear is an obstacle to our spiritual awakening. They assure us that when we become conscious of our deeper nature we'll no longer feel vulnerable. But in my experience this isn't true. When I'm conscious of the deep I, there's a deep knowing that I'm essentially safe, which is a great relief. But 'Tim' remains a vulnerable human being.

Knowing that I'm essentially safe doesn't take away my human vulnerability. It does the opposite. It allows me to fully acknowledge how fragile Tim is. When I'm deep awake I can dare to be vulnerable. I can remove the psychological suit of armour I wear to protect myself from the world. And this makes me feel tender and real. It opens my heart so I can connect with others in our shared vulnerability, which is the experience of kindness.

When I'm deep awake my human fears don't magically evaporate. Rather I can engage with the scary business of being human from the primal safety of my deepest being. I'm *both* frightened *and* not frightened at the same time. It's *both/and* not *either/or*.

When I was beginning my journey of awakening it was fashionable in spiritual circles to say that we had a choice to be governed by *either* fear *or* love. But this is a false dichotomy. To love is to fear for the ones we love. The more I love someone the more I'm concerned for their well-being. Love and fear are bedfellows not enemies.

Fear has got a bad name in spiritual circles, but fear isn't just bad. It can be a horribly debilitating experience, but it's also a natural part of the human condition. We're programmed by nature to be on the look out for predators … dangers … enemies. We could be killed at any moment and our instinctual nature is alert to this. We should be grateful for this fear.

As I mentioned previously I test the validity of spiritual teachings by asking if I'd share them with my children. So would I tell my children never to be fearful? Quite the opposite. As a parent I love my kids and fear they could get hurt. So I've taught them to be fearful of the cars in the road outside … of climbing too high on a tree that may not be secure … of trusting strangers who may not be as friendly as they seem.

Fear can be an appropriate response to a dangerous world, so seeing it as a spiritual enemy is absurd. I take a paralogical approach by being conscious of the essential safety of the deep I while also embracing my human vulnerability. Then I can dare to enter into the maelstrom of life, with all its ups and downs, surprises and disappointments, beginnings and endings. Seeing I'm essentially safe gives me the courage to really live.

Daring to Be Attached

Many spiritual traditions teach that to awaken we need to let go of our attachments. For years I tried to be unattached, but something in me resisted the idea. I presumed this was my ignorant ego struggling to prevent me awakening. But now it seems to me it was actually the voice of wisdom refusing to let me relinquish something so integral to my humanity.

The idea that attachments are bad is so common in spiritual circles that I used to presume it must be right. But then one day I became a father and everything changed. As I held my baby daughter in my arms for the first time I knew I was forever attached. I *wanted* to be attached to this tiny bundle of life. I wanted to be *so* attached that the bonds could never be broken.

In that moment I also saw clearly why attachment could cause me terrible suffering, because with great love comes great fear. I knew that if anything were to happen to this little girl it would break me in pieces. Yet I was willing to take this risk and love her anyway. I had no choice. My heart demanded it.

That's when I knew I was looking for a new approach to spirituality that honoured the poignant beauty of the personal life, rather than rejecting it as some sort of spiritual obstacle to be overcome. Our personal attachments give life its warmth and meaning. The idea that it would be more spiritual to be unattached now seems utterly absurd. It's the sort of idea that could only have been thought up by celibate men living in caves or monasteries … which is exactly what it is.

The absurdity of the teaching of non-attachment becomes clear to me when I ask myself if I'd teach my children to be unattached. When my little girl says to me, 'I love you, daddy', should I reply, 'That's nice but don't become attached'? I don't think so! I want her to feel attached to me and I want to feel attached to her. That's what it is to love each other.

It seems obvious to me that to be attached is both natural and desirable. It's a sign of how much I love that I'm willing to take the risk that attachment entails. I'm willing to suffer for love. And this doesn't seem foolish. It feels like a heroic response to the challenge of love.

When I'm deep awake it becomes possible to meet this challenge, because I'm conscious of *both* my human attachments *and* the deep I that is never attached. I see that I don't need to become unattached, because essentially I'm always unattached. The deep I is forever free.

When I'm deep awake I am *both* liberated from all attachments *and* willingly attached because of love. I am able to bear the fear that comes with my personal attachments, because I know that I am also free. So I can dare to love.

Our attachments hurt because we try to cling to someone or something in a world of impermanence. The great grief of life is that everything is fleeting. I will never be a young man again. I will never hold my baby daughter in my arms again. I will never argue with my deceased father again.

Yet impermanence is also the cause of great joy, because it means that every moment is a fresh expression of a new possibility. When we see the paradoxity of impermanence life becomes poignantly beautiful. Each moment becomes a blessing to be cherished before it passes forever. Every meeting becomes an opportunity to fall in love that will never come again.

Desire and Anger

Many spiritual traditions encourage us to avoid desire and anger, because we must simply accept things as they are. They teach us to eschew all the passions that disturb our calm equanimity. If we could only stop being so emotional we'd become spiritually awake. It seems to make sense, but does it really?

Acting from powerful passions can cause terrible suffering to others and ourselves. There's no denying the problem. But it seems to me that our natural emotions are only a problem when we're consumed by them. The solution is not to suppress our human nature. It's to be conscious of our deeper nature *as well*.

Desire is the fuel of life. Wanting things to be better pushes us forward to face new challenges. Passion is the spice of life. Feeling strong emotions wakes us up from the numbness of normality. Do we really need to sacrifice experiences that are integral to our humanity in order to wake up? I don't believe life is that perverse.

I would never tell my children that desire is a bad thing. I might tell them to stop wanting so much and to avoid coveting what they can't have. But I would never say that desire itself is bad. I want them to desire to experience more … to see and feel more … to understand more … to *be* more. So if I wouldn't tell my kids to stop desiring, why would I demand this of myself?

Neither would I tell my children that they shouldn't experience anger. I might ask them to tame their anger if it's out of control or to find a different response if the anger is inappropriate. But I'd never say that anger itself is bad. I want them to be angry when things aren't right. I want them to be able to defend themselves if they're being mistreated. I want them to feel outraged at the injustice in the world. So if I wouldn't tell my kids to never be angry, why would I demand this of myself?

Spiritual awakening is about becoming more loving. But being loving doesn't mean just being *nice.* To love is sometimes to be angry because of love. I've found as a parent that I can be angry and still love. There are times when I've needed to become angry with my kids to bring their attention to the way they are unconsciously behaving. Because I love them so much I want them to mature, even if it means temporarily they don't like me much.

Loving anger is a powerful emotion that propels me to compassionate action. I'm angry at all the needless suffering human beings cause each other, which fuels my desire to do something about the state of things. I'm angry that we tolerate so much unkindness in our culture, which makes me passionately insist we do something about it. Rage is sometimes the appropriate response to an outrageous world.

From a paralogical perspective there's no need to suppress our human emotions. We simply need to be *also* conscious of the serenity of the deep I. When I dive into the still depths I feel a primal peace. Then I see the paradoxity of my situation. On the surface there may be a passing storm, but at the depths I am always in love with things just as they are.

Pleasure and Lust

Traditional spirituality is often extremely disapproving of pleasure, which seems crazy to me. I'm a big fan of pleasure, but when I'm only superficially awake I only partially feel the enjoyment available to me, because I'm partly numb. When I'm deep awake I find myself really savouring the pleasures of life not avoiding them.

Lust is a passion that gets an especially bad press in spiritual circles. I can understand this because when we experience raw sexual desire it's very compelling. It can cause us to see the person we desire in a purely objective way, as a physical form that is eliciting an instinctual response. I know as a young man I felt terrible about my animal lust when it arose and I tried to suppress it.

Now it seems to me that, as with all the passions, the problem isn't lust. The problem is *just* lust. To see another human being merely as an object of our desire is to cut ourselves off from the depths of being within the other person and ourselves. But it's not an either/or situation. When lust arises along with love our animal urges can be exhilarating fun. Then we can *both* love the essence *and* lust after the appearance. Hurray for that!

In Greek mythology Aphrodite, the great goddess of love, was honoured as Urania, who represented spiritual love, and also as Porne the 'titillator'. I adore the inclusiveness of the ancient imagination. It encourages us to make space in our lives for our animal instincts, not to repress them in our zeal to be spiritually pure. It's inherent in the paradoxity of our identity that our essential nature is pure and simple, while our human nature is earthy and complex.

A Passionate Life

The deep I is always at peace even when the surface self is alive with passion. Our passions become a problem when we see only one pole of our paralogical identity. When we're conscious of all that we are, our human nature becomes something to celebrate not revile. What I love about artists is that they express and redeem our ambiguous humanity. What I find difficult about some spiritual teachers is that they make us feel bad about the way we naturally are.

I would hate to become a passionless person. I want to feel a fire burning in my belly. A yearning to live and express myself. A longing for a better world. I don't *just* want to feel at peace with life as it is. I *also* want to experience the tempestuous rush of new possibilities struggling within me to be born. I want to feel the heat of desire. The urgent pangs of hunger for more. The defiant will to grow.

WAKING UP AND ENTERING IN

When I'm deep awake I feel content to be human, with all of the struggles and suffering this necessarily entails. My human nature remains the same, but I'm also aware of the other paralogical pole of my identity. I'm *both* free from my humanity *and* engaged with my humanity at the same time. And this is not some spiritual feat I have to accomplish. It is simply being conscious of all that I am.

The more I'm conscious of the deep I, the more I can really enter into the story of Tim. When I'm only superficially awake I hold back from life because it's so scary. But in the deep awake state of safe vulnerability I'm able to take the risk and go for my life. I can dare to passionately engage with the frightening business of living. I can love being human.

CHAPTER 16

A THINKING PERSON'S GUIDE TO NOT THINKING

I'm a philosopher. I enjoy the discipline of clear thinking. I love the rush of sudden insight. Yet on my spiritual journey I've been told over and over again that my mind is a problem I need to overcome. I must stop thinking if I want to awaken. Yes … actually *stop* … completely!

I've been warned that the mind is a cunning adversary who will do anything to trick me out of awakening, because waking up entails the death of the mind. So the mind distracts me when I'm meditating. The mind fills me with mundane worries when I could be being spiritual. The mind makes me question the teachings of the master, when I should be unconditionally devotional.

It seems to me that this demonizing of the mind is a profound mistake. It's absolutely true, of course, that when we get lost in our habitual thoughts it makes it harder to awaken. This is a valuable insight, but it's only half the story. Thinking has a good side and a bad side … as everything does.

Treating the mind as just bad is a crazy idea, which people take seriously precisely because they're not thinking enough! As we've matured from children into adults we've worked hard to develop the ability to think, and here's some spiritual teacher telling us it's all been a colossal error. Surely that can't be right?!

Would I warn my kids, as I'm sending them off to school, that the mind is a problem and that they should do their best to stop thinking? Definitely not! I encourage my kids to think more not less. I want them to learn how to think clearly and imaginatively. I want them to develop a coherent understanding of life.

But I also want them to grasp the paradoxity of the mind. So I would explain to them that the mind is a great gift, yet it can cause all sorts of problems if we get carried away by the wrong thoughts. That's a both/and approach that works for me.

Struggling with the Mind

The demonizing of the mind makes it harder to awaken. If we become forever engrossed with battling the mind, this prevents us seeing how easy it is to wake up by simply becoming conscious of the thinker *as well as* the thoughts.

When we're told that we must silence the mind, yet it stubbornly continues to perform its thinking function, we blame ourselves for our failure. Or more accurately the mind starts to berate itself for its failure to stop being the mind! But the mind can't stop thinking any more than the heart can stop beating. That's what it does. And thank goodness for that. If the mind stopped thinking we wouldn't be enlightened … we'd be stupid!

The mind can seem like a spiritual adversary because when we're lost in the mind it's hard to be deep awake. But the mind isn't really the monster it's portrayed to be. When I examine the experience of thinking I find it's similar to talking. Thinking is imagining talking to myself within the privacy of my own psyche.

Just as it drives me mad when I'm with someone who won't stop talking, it also drives me mad when I won't stop talking to myself. I need to be quiet as well as talk. I need to be conscious of the deep silence as well as the ideas that arise within it. Then thinking isn't a problem. In fact, like a good conversation, it's a great pleasure.

Childish Spirituality

Believing that thinking is a hindrance on the journey of awakening leads to a regressive form of childish spirituality. Most of us are so embroiled with the complex responsibilities of the grown-up world that we long for the joyous simplicity of childhood, so this approach to spirituality can be very appealing. But it seems to me that it's disastrous.

When we reject the thinking mind we can enter a childlike state in which we too easily believe the most outrageous supernatural claims without reasonable doubt. We fall prey to predatory spiritual charlatans because we're looking for an all-knowing spiritual parent to look after us.

There is a childlike naïveté to many popular spiritual ideas. Let's look at some examples …

I don't need to be rational just to follow my intuition.

Great for spontaneous creativity, but rubbish for rocket science. What we need is to appreciate *both* the intuition *and* the rational mind.

Simply be in the moment, don't think about the past or the future.

Worth doing when you want to have fun, but not very helpful for learning from experience or planning new ventures. We need to pay attention *both* to the perpetual present *and* to our journey in time.

Everything will be alright because the universe will look after me.

Great for making you feel hopeful. But actually you *are* the universe and you need to look after yourself. The reality is that bad things happen to trusting people all the time. We need *both* to have faith in the essential goodness of life *and* to make sure we look after ourselves and each other.

In my experience when I'm deep awake I feel like a little child playing in the mystery. But I'm not *just* childlike. Being deep awake is not regressing to an earlier stage of my journey through life. It's progressing to a place where I can be *both* a thoughtful adult dealing with the challenges of life *and* like a child delighting in the present moment.

Being an adult without also being a child means we miss out on the joy of life. Being a child without also being an adult means we can't handle the practicalities of life. But we don't have to choose one or the other. We can be both at once. We can mature out of childhood into adulthood, yet remain conscious of our innocent heart which was there right from the start.

OUR THOUGHTS CREATE THE WORLD

From the paralogical perspective thinking is not the great spiritual problem it's made out to be. Actually it's absolutely essential to all of our experiences of life, including awakening, because it is the ability to frame concepts that allows us to be conscious at all.

An important Buddhist text called the *Dhammapada* begins:

With our thoughts we create the world.

There's an obvious way in which this is true.

Have a look around you and you'll see that everything you're conscious of you have a concept for.

I am doing this and I'm conscious of the computer screen … my office … the garden … the birdsong … the blue sky … the time of day … the coffee I'm drinking.

I'm conceptualizing everything I am conscious of.

My concepts divide up reality into 'this not that'. My coffee cup is 'this not that'. My computer keyboard is 'this not that'. The time of day is 'this not that'. I'm differentiating the world into comprehensible chunks and this is defining what I'm experiencing.

Our ideas allow us to discriminate reality into a multiplicity of things. But we're also discriminating the world without using words. There are pre-linguistic concepts that babies and animals possess that enable them to negotiate the world in simple ways.

When you chew a piece of meat in your mouth you're making an instinctual discrimination between the meat that is your food and the meat that is your tongue. And if you don't it hurts! (This is hard for me to imagine because I'm a life-long vegetarian, but it's such a good example I couldn't resist it.)

As we mature from children into adults we learn more and more concepts, which we use to divide up reality in ever more subtle ways. Through this process we steadily become more conscious of the world. As children we live in a small and simple world, but as adults we live in an enormous universe populated with an incredible diversity of separate things. That's because we're using a huge number of concepts to discriminate reality.

When we don't discriminate things we aren't conscious at all. This is the state of deep sleep. When we're awake we discriminate ourselves from the world as the subject of a stream of experience. Then we understand our experience by discriminating the world into individual things with different qualities.

So here's the big idea I want to share with you:

Consciousness is discrimination.

Consciousness arises as we discriminate the whole into separate parts. The more we discriminate the world the more conscious we become. It's discrimination that allows us to be conscious. So thinking isn't a spiritual error, because conceptualization is a prerequisite for us being conscious at all. And separateness isn't a trivial illusion, because it creates our conscious experience.

This leads us to an understanding of the profound paradoxity of awakening:

> We are only conscious because
> we're discriminating the world and
> creating separateness.

> And now we are conscious through separateness,
> we can *also* become conscious of the essential
> oneness of being.

Conscious Oneness

People often ask me, 'How can I be one with everything?' I playfully advise them to go to sleep, because in the deep sleep state there is only the oneness of unconscious being. This is an unsatisfactory answer, of course, because my questioner wants to spiritually awaken not go to sleep. But I like to use this question as an opportunity to point out the importance of separateness. Let me take you through it:

> Spiritual awakening is being *consciously*
> one with all.

The paradox is that consciousness arises with discrimination, so to be conscious is to experience separateness.

This means we can never *just* be conscious of oneness. We must become conscious of *both* separateness *and* oneness.

We must become conscious of the oneness *through* the separateness.

WHAT-IS BEFORE WORDS

We are conscious through discrimination, but if we want to wake up to oneness we must *also* pay attention to what-is before words. Let's do it now:

Ask yourself … what is the world before you think about it?

Ask yourself … who are you when you have no idea who you are?

CHAPTER 17

A LOVER OF LIFE

Since the influx of Indian philosophy into western culture in the last century, it's commonly assumed that spirituality is about aspiring to eradicate the ego and experience the state of enlightenment. I want to challenge this idea and suggest a new spiritual ideal to which we could aspire.

Enlightenment is often understood as the supreme state in which we're fully self-realized and permanently awake. Most people I meet don't really think they could ever achieve such an elevated state, but they often believe that some great master somewhere has made it to the winning post.

I no longer see the spiritual journey in this way. I don't aspire to arrive at some ultimate state. The idea of eradicating the ego seems misguided and holds no attraction. My experience of awakening makes me want to fully engage with the human adventure, not escape it. This has compelled me to conceptualize the spiritual ideal in a new way. I don't aspire to be an enlightened master, rather I aspire to be a humble 'lover of life'.

Becoming a 'lover of life' isn't about achieving a spiritually awakened state in which we're detached from life. It's becoming conscious of the deep I so that we can engage compassionately with the human adventure. It's discovering the love within us, so that we can express this love in the world around us.

When we become deep awake we discover the ocean of love that is our essential nature. But for me this isn't the end of the journey of awakening. Love by its very nature wants to be expressed. Love is *both* a feeling *and* an activity. It's in the nature of love to give of itself … to reach out from self to other … to create goodness in the world.

One of my favourite quotes is from the Gnostic *Gospel of Philip,* which explains:

> Those who are free through gnosis become slaves because of love.

This captures my experience of the paradoxity of awakening perfectly. When I deep know my essential nature I feel liberated from the confines of the story of Tim and conscious of the oneness of being. But the deep love I feel in the deep awake state impels me back into the story to compassionately engage with life … to care for others … to make the world a better place for future generations.

Know Yourself and Show Yourself

For me the journey of awakening is not just about transforming my state of consciousness, it's also about what I bring to life through the way I live. The enlightenment ideal pictures the purpose of spirituality as self-realization. I agree with this completely, because the journey of awakening leads us to become conscious of the deep I. But there's another, complementary pole to the paradoxity of awakening.

Spiritual awakening is also about self-expression. This means engaging with the process through which the separate self evolves, so that we can progressively express more of the infinite potential of our essential nature. It means entering into the creative process of life as a conscious collaborator with the primal being, to bring new possibilities into the world.

Self-realization and self-expression are complementary aspects of the adventure of awakening. Aspiring to become a lover of life means becoming conscious of *what we are* and bringing forth *what we can become.* It is loving ourselves the way we are and seeking to grow into a fuller expression of our potential.

Becoming a lover of life means reaching deep within so we can come further out. It means transcending the story so we can transform the story. It means daring to be a unique expression of the oneness of being, on a journey of self-realization and self-expression. It means both *knowing* ourselves and *showing* ourselves.

CAN WE ALWAYS BE DEEP AWAKE?

Many spiritual traditions suggest that the goal of the journey of awakening is to permanently inhabit some sublime super-conscious state. But it seems to me that this is simply not possible. The nature of consciousness is to constantly change. No two moments are ever the same. Consciousness is flux.

The idea that we could be permanently awake contradicts our actual experience. Every day we go through a cycle in which consciousness dissolves back into the primal ground of deep sleep and arises again refreshed. No one is permanently awake. Surely that's obvious?

Consciousness is like a wave that rises and falls. Sometimes we're extremely energized and more conscious, other times we're tired and less conscious. The process of awakening doesn't lead to a permanently awake state, because it's the nature of consciousness to come and go. The primal ground of being is always present, but our experience of it must change.

Every day we move between the sleeping, dreaming and waking states. Spirituality can help us add the deep awake state to this cycle. As we arise from sleeping into waking we can expand consciousness further to become deep awake. Then we can surf the wave of consciousness as it rises and falls from deep sleep to deep awake.

If we make it our goal to be permanently awake we will inevitably fail. If we blame that failure on our spiritual immaturity or the evil ego we will feel increasingly bad about ourselves. Rather than coming to love ourselves as we are, we'll constantly confirm our deepest fear … that we aren't good enough.

Embracing the spiritual ideal of becoming a 'lover of life' doesn't mean aspiring to the impossible goal of always being deep awake. It means loving our experience of life as it actually is. It means accepting that consciousness inevitably rises and falls, because that's inherent in the paralogical nature of life. It means understanding that we must experience being *less* conscious to experience being *more* conscious.

AN EVOLUTIONARY JOURNEY

Life is evolving. The universe is an ongoing creative process, through which the infinite potential of being is progressively actualizing. Each one of us is an evolving fragment of the cosmos. This idea of evolution has become central to our modern understanding of existence. Yet many forms of spirituality are rooted in the distant past before this understanding had arisen. This means we need to update our spiritual ideas so that we conceive of awakening as a perpetual process of evolution, rather than an end-driven dash for ultimate salvation.

I want to suggest that the purpose of the spiritual journey is not to arrive anywhere, but rather to engage with the adventure of life in a new way, so that the evolutionary process unfolds powerfully within us. It's about waking up to our deeper *being* so that we can more fully engage with the evolutionary adventure of *becoming* a more conscious individual. It's about living our lives as a transformational process through which we are learning to love.

This is not a linear process in which we steadily become more awake. It's a paralogical process that entails finding ourselves and losing ourselves … wonderful insight and deep confusion … great elation and harrowing suffering. The spiritual challenge is to willingly enter into the transformative maelstrom of life.

Travelling and Arriving

The spiritual journey is an evolutionary process. There are stages of realization which we can reach, but there's no final destination, because there's always further to go. My journey was initiated by the realization that it's possible to experience the deep awake state. At some point I became conscious of the deep I that transcends Tim. Then I recognized that at the depths of life there is no separateness and all is one.

These realizations and many others have been stages on my journey of awakening. But the evolutionary adventure shows no sign of slowing up, let alone coming to completion. Each new level of understanding I arrive at leads inexorably to the next challenge. Life is always a paralogical dance of *both* arriving *and* travelling.

The most important realization for me, which was there right at the start and has remained with me throughout my journey, is that what really matters is love. It's this realization that has freed me from the desire to arrive at some final spiritual destination and led me to embrace the ever-changing challenges of my life as opportunities to continually grow in love. It's this realization that has led me to adopt the spiritual ideal of becoming a 'lover of life'.

THE INCONSTANT LOVER

Many people seem to think that the journey of awakening is about achieving some sort of spiritual perfection. But I want to suggest that to be human is necessarily to be imperfect. We all have our flaws and foibles. Everyone who can walk sometimes stumbles. The best musicians still hit bum notes.

Becoming a lover of life is accepting that it's only human to err. We are unconscious *being* in the process of *becoming* conscious. No surprise, therefore, that we spend so much time groping around in semi-conscious darkness. When we understand this we can be patient with ourselves and our fellow travellers on the journey of life.

To aspire to become a lover of life isn't to fantasize about becoming a spiritual superman. Quite the opposite. It's acknowledging that there can be no evolution unless there's always something missing and more to discover. It's embracing the glorious imperfection of personal existence. It's creatively engaging with the ambiguity of being human.

To aspire to become a lover of life is to aspire to become wise by accepting we'll sometimes be foolish. It's recognizing that we'll always make mistakes because of our lack of consciousness. This is the process of evolution. If we didn't err we'd never learn. And if we didn't learn we'd never grow. Indeed, it seems to me, if we're not continually making mistakes we're getting too comfortable and should be taking more risks!

To become a lover of life we must be willing to be a foolish lover … a lost lover … a vulnerable lover … a lonely lover … a broken lover … a frightened lover … a flawed lover … an inconstant lover. We must be willing to love being human with all that this entails.

LOVING BEING AND BEING LOVING

Becoming a lover of life involves adopting a paralogical approach to awakening.

> It means becoming conscious of the deep I and *loving being*.

> Then expressing this love in the world by *being loving*.

The essence of how to live a deep awake life is to practise 'loving being and being loving', so that we *both* awake to the deep I *and* compassionately engage with the adventure of life. This paralogical practice is the beating heart of the new way of awakening I've been exploring with you. But essentially the same idea is also found in many spiritual traditions. The great Tibetan sage Milarepa teaches that the essence of Buddhism is:

> Know emptiness.
> Be compassionate.

We need to become conscious of our essential nature as the spacious presence of awareness, so we deep know that all is one, and find ourselves in love with all. Then we need to express that love by living compassionately.

The same message is also at the heart of the Christian tradition. When Jesus is asked, 'What is the greatest commandment?' he replies:

> Love God with all your heart. This is the first and greatest commandment.

> And the second is like it: Love others as yourself.

The first commandment is to love God, which means communing with the primal oneness of being. The second commandment is to love others as yourself, because when you wake up to oneness you see that others *are* your self. These two commandments are like each other, because they are paralogically complementary perspectives on the spiritual journey, which involves *loving being* and *being loving*.

THE NEW SPIRITUAL IDEAL

Do you resonate with my suggestion for a new spiritual ideal? Do you also aspire to be a lover of life? Here's the paralogical essence of what that means:

> Being a lover of life means waking up to oneness and passionately engaging with your individual journey through life.

It means being open to the present moment as a precious opportunity to experience the richness of life and feel its transformative power.

It means seeing life as an evolutionary adventure and welcoming the challenges through which you grow as a person.

It means embracing your flawed humanity and accepting that you will stumble on the journey of life … that you become wise by being foolish … that you can't always be awake and at your best.

It means immersing yourself in the deep love and then learning to express that love more expansively and inclusively in the world.

It means knowing yourself and showing yourself, by expressing your secret potential so that the world is richer for you being here.

It means loving your life as it is while working for a better future.

CHAPTER 18

THE HEROIC LOVER

Some approaches to spirituality make it sound as if life is a breeze. If we could just be more spiritual we'd sail through life, borne forward by the winds of grace towards an ever more wonderful horizon. But we all know that life isn't like that. Life can be tough. We all suffer. We all face obstacles that we feel we'll never be able to surmount. We feel despair as well as elation. We feel defeated as well as empowered.

Aspiring to be a lover of life doesn't mean hoping that the sun will always shine. Quite the opposite. Becoming a lover of life means finding the courage to meet life with love, even when all seems lost … *especially* when all seems lost!

Being a lover of life means becoming a human hero on the adventure of a lifetime. The fact that life can be so bitter and cruel demands a heroic response. The experience of impermanence and loss demands a heroic response. The unkindness and callousness of others demands a heroic response. The knowledge that we will die demands a heroic response.

To be a lover of life is to be a heroic lover on a sacred quest to become an embodiment of love. This means facing the dilemmas that confront us with bold determination to love. But the hero doesn't start triumphant, win every war and return victorious. The hero struggles and fails, yet finds the inner strength to come back from defeat and love again.

The word 'quest' comes from the same root as 'question'. To be a heroic lover is to ask a deep question of life: *what are you?* And in return to be asked: *who are you?* Through undertaking the adventure of life the heroic lover discovers who they are. And they find they're stronger than they imagined. Their inner resources are deeper than they thought.

The heroic lover understands that the challenges they face are mighty. They humbly acknowledge that life can lift them up and cast them down. They know that if they aren't humble they will be humbled. And with that knowledge they step valiantly forth on the adventure of love.

In the ancient world the word 'hero' referred to someone who was devoted to the goddess Hera, who set the hero their challenges. To be a heroic lover is to be devoted to the goddess of life. It is welcoming the trials she sets us, through which we can become worthy of her love ... the heroic feats she demands of us through which we can prove our devotion ... the storms we must endure to chisel beautiful lines of wisdom into our unformed features.

Enjoying and Enduring

Life is to be enjoyed *and* endured. That's one of the great paradoxities the heroic lover must understand. When we enjoy life it feels good. When we endure life it deepens our wisdom and compassion. To 'endure' is to become 'durable', which means to become strong. And life wants us to become strong, so we can withstand the storms as well as delight in the sunshine. So we can love whatever the weather.

Often we attempt to endure the trials of life by becoming hard and defended, or numb and withdrawn. The spiritual challenge is to bear the suffering without closing our hearts. More than this ... it's letting the suffering open us up.

Suffering is awful, but it can awaken us just as much as joy and wonder. The heroic lover is ready to be shaken up so that they can be shaken free. They understand the lover's heart must break open at some time … maybe many times … for love to flow.

The heroic lover endures the suffering of life, because they know that dark periods transform into golden days. They hold on to hope when life seems meaningless, because they know that it will become meaningful later. When the night comes they don't despair, because they know the dawn will follow.

Enduring the trials of life isn't easy. But as Joseph Campbell, the great mythologist and champion of the heroic life, writes:

> If you are lifeworthy, you can take it. What we are really living for is the experience of life, both the pain and the pleasure.

The heroic lover accepts the pain of life and relishes the pleasure. They endure tenderly and enjoy passionately. They're prepared to suffer the grind that polishes away their rough edges and they're hungry for every sweet moment that comes their way. They feast on the bittersweet banquet of life.

Diving and Surfing

If you put a yin/yang symbol on its side it becomes an image of an undulating wave. This is a wonderful image, because our experience of life is like a wave rising and falling between joy and suffering ... ease and struggle ... consciousness and unconsciousness.

The spiritual challenge is to surf the wave. To do this we must first dive into the depths of the ocean of being. When our point of balance is rooted in the depths we can surf the wave on the surface of life. When we're conscious of the primal goodness of being we can live with our ups and downs.

To surf the wave as it rises and falls we need to pay attention *both* to the perpetual now *and* to where we're travelling in time. If we only pay attention to where we hope or fear the story is going, we'll misjudge the wave as it crashes through the present and lose our balance.

When this happens we find ourselves drowning not surfing. But the heroic lover understands that learning to surf means frequently falling off the wave. They know that real success is constantly coming back from failure.

The heroic lover accepts that life is characterized by paradoxity, which means that their experience always flows between good and bad. They don't dream of one without the other. They surf the wave up and down through despair and hope … failure and success … grief and ecstasy.

THE WOUNDED LOVER

The heroic lover is also a wounded lover. No one makes it through the trials of life without being wounded on the way. Everyone carries the scars of the hurt they've endured. We're all damaged goods.

If our flesh is wounded it will hopefully heal, but this may still leave a scar that can easily be aggravated into an open wound. I want to suggest that, in a similar way, the psychological wounds we've suffered leave scars on the soul which can be easily opened.

We all have soul wounds left by painful experiences. Often we suffer soul wounds when we're at our most vulnerable as children. For some of us the wounds heal but leave a scar that is tender when touched. For others these wounds are so deep they never completely heal.

The Cycle of Suffering

When our physical wounds are irritated we instinctively react to protect our broken body from further harm. In the same way when our soul wounds are irritated it can hurt so much that we lash out in protective anger. We may behave in brutish ways that arise from an animal instinct to avoid pain.

This can lead to terrible conflict in our relationships, because it often creates a cycle of suffering, which leaves everyone sore. I know there have been countless times in my life when I've irritated someone's soul wound and they've reacted with psychological violence to protect themselves … which has aggravated one of my own soul wounds and this has made me react aggressively to protect myself … and this reaction has opened up the other person's wound deeper, so they've reacted … so then I've reacted … and the cycle of suffering rolls on.

Understanding that soul wounds are similar to physical wounds helps me break the cycle of suffering. It enables me to bring understanding to the conflicts I experience. I stop being angry with others because they are sore. I stop blaming myself for being wounded.

Just as deep sleep heals the body, so being deep awake heals the soul. When we bring deep love to our psychological wounds miracles can happen. But just as no amount of sleep can heal every physical wound, deep awake healing can't mend every fracture of the heart. This means we need to learn to be gentle with those parts of the psyche that are most inflamed.

One of the greatest challenges we face is to live tenderly with our soul wounds and the soul wounds of others, so that we ameliorate rather than aggravate our suffering. We've all been hurt by life and carry the scars. So we need to be kind and take care of each other.

CHAPTER 19

THE TRANSFORMATIONAL DRAMA

How many films have there been that start with all going well, progress with everything working out, and end happily ever after? We don't want to watch a story like that. We want tension and drama … misfortune and humour … catharsis and transformation … chaos and resolution. We want a story that moves us to feel something. A story that leaves us richer for the telling.

Comedy relieves us from the burden of being too serious, so that we can play in the moment. Yet a romantic comedy with no bite becomes sentimental and sickly. Tragedy reminds us of the gravity of life, so that we can feel compassion and empathy. Yet a harrowing tragedy with no redemption becomes dark and bitter. We want the paralogical play of opposites in our stories. And that's what we've got with the great tragicomedy of life.

The story of life is a dramatic narrative through which the hero is transformed. Much of the time our lives may feel ordinary and orderly, but sooner or later the chaos of life explodes us out of our comfort zone. Then life ceases to be a safe routine and becomes a grand adventure.

To be a lover of life means welcoming this call to take up a new quest for deeper wisdom and greater love. It means facing the challenges we confront, even when we fear we'll fail, because we know that within us lie the limitless resources of the primal being. It's having faith in love to sustain us through our trials, knowing that we'll be richer for the ordeal.

To be a lover of life is not to turn away from the reality of suffering … failure … breakdown … horror … illness … old age … death. It's embracing those aspects of life we don't like and don't want to acknowledge. If we can take love into those places that seem unlovable, we'll truly come to be a lover of life … all of life … life as it is.

To be a lover of life means daring to be a vulnerable, tender, wounded human being on a heroic adventure of learning to love. Becoming a lover of life means welcoming the moment whether it brings transcendent bliss or gritty transformation. Becoming a lover of life means saying 'yes' to your life.

LIFE IS ALWAYS GOOD

We need to accept that our experience of life is *both* good *and* bad. Some traditional approaches to spirituality offer the dream of overcoming suffering. Some modern approaches to spirituality promise a perfect life if we use the power of positive intentions. I feel there is something to be learned from both ideas. Yet I feel they can also be extremely misleading.

Existence is predicated on paradoxity, so our experience flows between good and bad, joy and suffering, yum and yuk. We hope for yum without yuk. We fear there will be yuk without yum. But there is always both. We can focus on the good, but we can't exile the bad. We can make our lives better, but we can't make our lives perfect.

Buying into the fantasy that we could have yum without yuk leads to profound disappointment and confusion. We're attempting the impossible, so we inevitably fail. Then we blame ourselves for not being spiritually awake enough to create the perfect life we long for. But actually we're not at fault. It's the unrealistic idea that we can have good without bad that is at fault.

When we face challenges in our lives we think of them as problems. But they are *also* opportunities to learn and grow, so that we become more awake and loving. Nothing that happens is *just* bad and nothing is *just* good. Life is always *both* good *and* bad, depending on how we look at it.

Even at the best of times there are things we wish were different. Even at the worst of times there are things we wouldn't change. If we look at life paralogically with both eyes open, we can see every moment as *both* good *and* bad. Good and bad exist within each other, like yin and yang on the *taijitu* symbol, where within the light is a dot of dark and within the dark is a dot of light.

So the bad news is that there's always something bad about life we can choose to focus on.

And the good news is that there's always something good about life we can choose to focus on.

Life may be yuk, but it's never *just* yuk. The world remains a marvel to be wondered at. There's always the delicious feeling of breathing. There's always the joy of simply being. There's always hope for a better tomorrow.

Life may be bad, but it's always good! This means that when times are bad we can seek out the good that is also present. Then, in the words of Walt Whitman, we see that:

> What is called good is perfect
> and what is called bad is just as perfect.

In my experience when I see it's all perfect I can embrace my life as it is. It's also imperfect of course. I could give you a long list of things that could be better. But the imperfections of my life are also perfect. It's the grit that creates the pearl.

LOVING YOUR LIFE

Whoever you are and whatever your story, your life is amazing precisely because it is *your* life. You are the hero of the story, who has had to face the trials and tribulations every hero must face. You've felt triumphant and humbled. You've been admired and condemned. You've been happy and disconsolate.

You've felt numb and enlivened. But through it all you have been *you*. Joseph Campbell reminds us:

> The privilege of a lifetime is being who you are.

I've been thinking about my own journey through life. What a paradoxical adventure it has been. At times so beautiful and yet so cruel. So exhilarating yet so suffocating. So intoxicating yet so sobering. So *everything!* I feel flooded with poignant memories:

> I've held my newborn baby girl for the first time and been engulfed by an ocean of love. I've watched my father struggle to move his paralyzed body and listened to his guttural groans of 'help, help, help'.

> I've gazed across a dancing circle at a young woman dressed in wedding white and known I would love her forever. I've felt my heart crack open and been flooded with despair hearing the words 'I'm leaving'.

> I've walked in grace and every accidental encounter has seemed charged with significance. I've stood alone in the night and felt the meaningless chill of the endless void.

I've slept side by side with my lover and known a peace beyond understanding. I've awoken in the dark, sweating with fear, and utterly alone.

What about you? Is that how it's been for you?

I've sat in meditation with no financial security and few possessions, and had more than enough. I've become so stressed about making money I've made myself ill.

I've indulged myself with luxury in a 5-star spa, like a king who deserves only the best. I've stared from a hotel window in Delhi at a family living in a waste pipe and wept with shame.

I've strolled through verdant woods and felt one with nature's beauty. I've watched a dog tear a weasel to pieces and been horrified at nature's casual brutality.

I've been numb with the relentless repetition of mundane life … the eating and excreting … the wearing and the washing. I've been shocked to feel blissfully happy for no reason at all while clearing the dishes or making the bed.

I've seen astonishing miracles that have filled me with faith and marvelled at the perfection of all that occurs. I've seen a horrible fate befall honourable people and railed against the blows of capricious chance.

You too, I'm guessing?

I've run naked in the rain through the city night in reckless ecstasy. I've crouched in the corner of a disused bandstand, tired and lost, drinking whisky with a friend.

I've desired a woman's beautiful body because it was the most exquisite thing I'd ever seen. I've been conscious of myself as a mortal meat-bag and become nauseated by my raw physicality.

I've known someone so well I could feel what they were thinking. Then I've discovered I didn't know them at all.

I've known who I am with confident certainty. Then found dark things within me that I cannot confess.

I've been elated by triumph and belligerent with hope. I've cuddled down with my broken dreams and wished for unbroken sleep.

Have you felt the same? Have you heard the soaring highs and rumbling lows of the symphony of life?

I've been with a friend eaten away by cancer who's smiled while he confided he was actually enjoying the experience of dying. I've seen a friend become a millionaire and lose the joy of living.

I've known passionate purpose turn to disheartened resignation. I've known crippling depression transform into euphoric renewal.

I've laughed so hard it's become agonizing pleasure. I've cried so tenderly my tears have dissolved my despair.

I've been open-heartedly optimistic about human creativity and our collective awakening to oneness and love. I've been hard-headedly pessimistic about human depravity and feared an impending collapse into chaos and division.

I have surfed the waves of hope and despair as they have risen and fallen.

And looking back on it all, I can say this …

I love my life.

CHAPTER 20

DEEP SELF-EMPOWERMENT

So this is where our journey ends. In this book I've presented a paralogical approach to awakening that encourages us to wake up to oneness *and* celebrate separateness … to be conscious of the deep I *and* embrace our flawed humanity … to know deep peace *and* feel intense passions … to play in the moment *and* evolve through time.

My greatest hope is that having spent this time together you feel inspired to become a lover of life … to be the hero of your story … to passionately enter into the bittersweet drama. I want you to feel self-empowered from the depths of your being, so you can feel the creative energy of the universe pouring through you. I want you to be confident that you can make a difference to the world, because you can feel the awesome power of love within you.

Here we are. You and me and everyone. All on this astonishing journey of life. Each one of us is a unique expression of the oneness of being. Each one of us is an imperfect human being. And when we feel the deep love we can embrace ourselves and each other as we are. We can commune in love and care for one another. We can hold each other by the hand and walk each other home.

When I am deep awake it's obvious that love is what really matters in life. I recently came across a wonderful quote from Professor Jacques Decour that really speaks to the importance of love in a very inspiring way. He was executed by the Nazis at the age of 32 for his activity in the French resistance during the Second World War. As he was waiting for death he wrote a beautiful letter to his family, which includes this extraordinarily moving passage:

> Now each of us is preparing to die. We are thinking about what is to come, about what is going to kill us without our being able to do anything to defend ourselves. This is truly the

moment for us to remember love. Did we love enough? Did we spend hours a day marvelling at other people, being happy together, feeling the value of contact, the weight and the worth of hands, eyes, bodies? Do we really know how to devote ourselves to tenderness?

Before we pass away in the trembling of an earth without hope, it is time to become entirely and definitely love, tenderness and friendship, because there is nothing else. We must swear to think of nothing anymore but loving, opening our souls and our hands, looking with our best eyes, clasping what we love tightly to ourselves, walking free from anxiety and radiant with affection.

In my final hours, when I look back at all that has happened, I know it will be the love that I've given and received that will really matter. Do you feel the same? I remember the breathless words of my father on the night he died, reaching out from his depths with such determination:

Tell everyone how much I love them.

It's impossible to capture the sincerity of a dying man.

The Wonder of Your Life

Our lives are so precious. You and I are unique human beings who have never existed before and will never exist again. We are living lives that have never been lived before and will never be lived again. So let's play our parts in the great drama with style and panache.

Among all the drudgery and broken dreams, what makes life worth all the fuss? The great lover of life Walt Whitman answers:

> That you are here – that life exists, and identity;
> That the powerful play goes on, and you will contribute a verse.

So let's sing that verse with passionate intensity. Let's hold our own note and create new harmonies within the symphony of life.

Life is such an amazing show, how could we not want to be a part of it? It's all so miraculous. Indeed science has shown that if the fundamental nature of the universe were infinitesimally different, then life would have been impossible. Do you know what the chances are of a universe existing in which we could be here contemplating this question?

The eminent mathematician and physicist Sir Roger Penrose has worked it out as 1 in 100, 000, 000, 000, 000, 000, 000, 000, 000, 000, 000, 000, 000, 000, 000, 000, 000, 000, 000, 000, 000, 000, 000, 000, 000, 000, 000, 000, 000, 000, 000, 000, 000, 000, 000, 000, 000, 000, 000, 000, 000, 000, 000, 000, 000, 000, 000, 000, 000, 000, 000, 000, 000, 000, 000, 000, 000, 000, 000, 000, 000, 000, 000, 000, 000, 000, 000, 000, 000, 000, 000, 000, 000, 000, 000, 000!

Doesn't that make you feel lucky? Doesn't it fill you with awe and gratitude? Doesn't it make you appreciate the wonder of life? As the American poet e.e. cummings writes:

> i thank You God for most this amazing
> day: for the leaping greenly spirits of trees
> and a blue true dream of sky; and for everything
> which is natural which is infinite which is yes

The Buddha once said:

> If you could see the miracle of a single flower clearly, your whole life would change.

During one of his sermons he was silent and held out a flower before him. His student Mahākāśyapa began to laugh. He awoke in that moment and his life was never the same.

I hold up this moment before you to wonder.

If you see what a miracle this moment is your life will change.

It will be WOW.

THE DEEP AWAKENING

If you want to continue our journey together I invite you to join me at *The Deep Awakening,* which is a sublime mix of spiritual retreat and celebration of life. There's a magic that happens when we're present together in the same place, so come and dive into the deep love with me.

If you join me for this adventure it is my intention that you experience the WOW of awakening so powerfully that things will never be the same again. I want you to return home conscious and connected, having shared a very special experience with some amazing new friends … ready to live a deep awake life.

www.TimFreke.com

Visit my website for information about events, more books, audio guided meditations and free access to an archive of talks and interviews.

MORE BOOKS BY T!M FREKE

Soul Story
Evolution and the self-realizing universe

Lucid Living
Experience your life like a lucid dream

The Mystery Experience
A revolutionary approach to spiritual awakening

How Long Is Now?
How to be spiritually awake in the real world

In the Light of Death
Spiritual insights on death and bereavement

The Jesus Mysteries
Was the original Jesus a pagan god?

The Hermetica
The lost wisdom of the pharaohs

WATKINS

Sharing Wisdom Since
1893

The story of Watkins dates back to 1893, when the scholar of esotericism John Watkins founded a bookshop, inspired by the lament of his friend and teacher Madame Blavatsky that there was nowhere in London to buy books on mysticism, occultism or metaphysics. That moment marked the birth of Watkins, soon to become the home of many of the leading lights of spiritual literature, including Carl Jung, Rudolf Steiner, Alice Bailey and Chögyam Trungpa.

Today, the passion at Watkins Publishing for vigorous questioning is still resolute. Our wide-ranging and stimulating list reflects the development of spiritual thinking and new science over the past 120 years. We remain at the cutting edge, committed to publishing books that change lives.

DISCOVER MORE . . .

Read our blog

Watch and listen to
our authors in action

Sign up to
our mailing list

JOIN IN THE CONVERSATION

 WatkinsPublishing    @watkinswisdom

 watkinsbooks   watkinswisdom    watkins-media

Our books celebrate conscious, passionate, wise and happy living.
Be part of the community by visiting

www.watkinspublishing.com